Other Books By PJ Karr, Ph.D.

Spellbound
A Memoir

2019 Archway Publishing
www.archwaypublishing.com

Cliffhangers
Dramas and The Renaissance

2017 Archway Publishing
www.archwaypublishing.com

I Never Stopped…

2016 Archway Publishing
www.archwaypublishing.com

Daring Divas

2015 Archway Publishing
www.archwaypublishing.com

Tango On
Attitude = Altitude

2014 Archway Publishing
www.archwaypublishing.com

Catchin' the Sun and Moonbeams, Dad…
Play, Laugh, Love

2013 Archway Publishing
www.archwaypublishing.com

40 Ways to Stretch Your Smileage

2011 Dorrance Publishers

AHA Epiphanies to Release
the Spirit Within

2009 Dorrance Publishers

EPIPHANIES

Muses And Revelations For Mindful Connections,
Re-Awakenings, And Our Harmony

PJ Karr, Ph.D.

ARCHWAY
PUBLISHING

Archway Publishing books may be ordered through booksellers or by contacting:

Archway Publishing
1663 Liberty Drive
Bloomington, IN 47403
www.archwaypublishing.com
1 (888) 242-5904

Interior Image Credit: PJ Karr, Ph.D.

ISBN: 978-1-4808-9211-8 (sc)
ISBN: 978-1-4808-9212-5 (e)

Library of Congress Control Number: 2020911451

Print information available on the last page.

Archway Publishing rev. date: 08/13/2020

Dedication

To the individuals—our front-liners—befriending our planet...
  who share their gifts, talents, and ingenious thinking so that our world moves towards a synchronistic balance, a rejuvenation, and the unity

To the impassioned women, men, adolescents, and children...
  who offer their generosity, loving-kindness, and inspiration to significant others, acquaintances, and strangers, without any expectations of reciprocation or the accolades

To the unsung heroines and heroes...
  whose humanitarian efforts and stories do not appear frequently in the limelight of our global world and the breaking news

To endearing Madre and JJ...
  who believed and shared what our world often desires—love, sweet love

Table of Contents

Acknowledgments

I was beholden to my standout buddies—John and Marty. As my ultimate and in-the-big-league friends, they were the allies who "hung with ya!" across the decades, especially during any of the rollercoaster rides.

Their salient advocacy of PJ's writing endeavors was uncommon. Their brilliance was a "rare combo" of the IQ and EQ. Yes, they were smarties. Yes, they were pals who were capable of dropping that incredible 13 inches from their IQ brains to their EQ hearts. Compassion and humanitarian efforts reigned sovereign with my exceptional comrades.

John and Molly at Gallery 55 flung open the vintage doors to us, the zany and earnest prose writers, storytellers, and musicians. The studio was relaxing with comfy couches, delightful yummies, and eclectic art displays. From the New England foliage days of October to the budding, flourishing days of May, John and Molly welcomed each of us. They offered an unequivocal acceptance—in our world often riddled with the confining expectancies and strait-laced critiques.

My sister-friend Vero from a yearly, holistic conference volunteered her dilettantish haven near Manhattan, New York. Her bungalow-chalet was in a quaint village that housed exquisite artists, studios, boutiques, and the organic farm-to-table eateries. My early books and penning the PJ messages for intriguing patrons resonated in Vero's inclusive bungalow.

The lovely Five— dynamic, talented, and charismatic women— the enterprising owners of the Five Crows that juried and featured all of my books. Their metro west network near Boston was high-powered. A mere thanks to these supportive and influential women would never be enough.

Of course, the "creatives" at the Apple store in Massachusetts were touted for years. My training sessions with these talented geeks and geekettes were over the top. Most importantly, each techno-wizard grasped how to tutor and open the eyes of the masses who possessed such variant learning styles. The rave reviews and gratitude were still forthcoming, as I had not forsaken my Apple training sessions nor the lofty learning curves.

Earth angels who emerged as eloquent and expressive messengers—Anna, Norma Star, Angela, Ross, Arlene, Morgan, and Lilly—thank you became a trite expression for your intuition and savvy insights. Your attributes of superlative giving and perceptiveness did not go unnoticed or unappreciated. Namaste!

As always, there were my ethereal guides who spawned the spiritual offerings of "knowing and not knowing." The butterflies, dragonflies, cloud images, and talking-moons kept evolving as the PJ mainstays. Their lauded and metaphysical messages generated my unexpected moments of enlightenment.

No mystification as to why the "PJ thanksgiving" kept amplifying. Wayne Dyer, Eckhart Tolle, Deepak Chopra, Elizabeth Gilbert, Maya Angelou, Marianne Williamson, and other spirit-filled authors permitted my cup to runneth over and the mindfulness to thrive.

Dalai Lama, Tibetan White and Green Tara, male yogi and female yogini, and Sat Nam were not contrived in my personal transformation. Being exposed to the glorious masters and the awe-inspiring heritage became my evolving legacy, not to be taken for granted.

Since the inception and almost-completed compositions for this book, our "world pandemic" was now catapulting on a daily basis. Attempts to give future forecasts and how to deal with all of "the unknowns" were equally prominent.

Humanitarian deeds with diverse individuals and our personal efforts offered the daily glimmers and traces of hope, the optimism, and an inner solace. My acknowledgment and gratitude of these good deeds resonated each day, week, and across the months.

No matter what we witnessed or heard as despair or hopelessness, we searched courageously for the alternative paths and feasible resolutions. Inevitably, each of our souls was still being touched in the most unique and unforgettable ways.

Introduction

I digress momentarily. I know what I wrote a year ago. I was scheduling a valuable part of my annual medical examination. Today, these front-line doctors, nurses, and health professionals are confronted with our "new normal" and only the "essential and emergency" needs. They have given wholeheartedly to at-risk individuals affected by our global pandemic.

Today's uncharted territories were not even imagined or envisioned by these doctors, health professionals, or myself. I digress again to these flashbacks of what was a different reality for all of us—not so long ago.

It was the two-year scheduling of my bone density scan. Once again, the fascinating machine and its fluid motion would reveal the proactive findings for my well being. That day, I found myself pausing purposefully. I was inquisitive. Our astronomical brains were actually like this innovative techno-scanner.

Hallelujah. My synapses in my young-elder brain were *still* traversing, much like this bone density scanner. An innate desire for my epiphanies was housed within the to-and-fro branches of my brain. Hopefully, the PJ synapses would bring forth the brand-new muses and the "aha" revelations.

Why not? I adopted the self-indulgent realm of positive thinking. *PJ brain scanner, please bequeath the PJ goodies. New epiphanies, if you please.* My "aha" moments and flourishing ideas for epiphanies branched out and arrived. Hmm, they were not exactly on cue.

Across a few years, the phenomenon of my "aha" moments transformed. I had been reading the credible authors for a longer duration. There was a growing body of research, awareness, and an increased societal acceptance about the personal shifts and our renewals.

Like-minded individuals shared these experiences of their "aha" moments and the re-awakenings at speeches, workshops, and retreats. I overheard similar conversations when I was traveling—for a reason. Other months, the "aha" was a look-see from my patio chair to the conservation land when a "new moment" just appeared.

The uncanny and new "aha" moments happened. Creative introspections went "kerplunk" in the PJ brain scanner. Different months or years, it was my travels that became the flashback, like a vivid and uncanny replay of a movie.

These unforeseen triggers helped to induce my novel branches and the contemporary brain synapses. Aha! I experienced an enhanced focus, given the sparks of mindfulness and quality time for composing these popping epiphanies.

My I-phone dictation or notes "app" plus my scribbles on notepads were the convincing "hooks." As an avid writer, I jotted down each endowment. Eventually, I transferred these teeming, bubbling epiphanies or percolating muses onto my trusty MacBook Air computer.

No worries! Ideas began to meld naturally with a theme that matched my random surprises. Yes, we writers are smitten with the incidental surprises that evolve into our computer nuggets.

An imprinting of images gave birth to my engaging pathways. My brain scanner began to work while I waited in grocery or pharmacy lines. There was no boredom or irritation with these stick-around lines, but rather a growing acceptance of my arousing imprinting.

Have you noticed? Trust me, none of us has to be a curious or wannabe writer to become immersed.

Take a few moments. Recall how you used to glance when you sauntered by a store window or the boutiques? Phrases abounded on the decorative walls, distressed furniture, or other gifts for contemporary homesteads. Epiphanies appeared regularly on posters and t-shirts. My memories caused the flashbacks.

I published an earlier chapbook entitled, "AHA: Epiphanies to Release the Spirit Within." The requests came for my weekly "aha posts" in the foyer of my fitness center.

Men and women of all ages and cultures expressed a desire for additional epiphanies. People sought out the fitness manager. Where was the author? They were inspired, wondering if Dr. PJ worked out at this gym. The manager was excited to share their commentaries.

"She made my day with this week's quote." "I want to have a *new* AHA each day that I enter the door for my workout." "These sayings inspire me to reflect, smile, or just try to be a better person that day." "I would like to meet her and tell her how she influenced my day."

Time to zoom forward a decade from that chapbook. None of us were affected by a global pandemic or envisioned anything like the "new normal." People were living their life—full of work, family, college, hobbies, travel, and whatever.

I was writing this new book, enamored and compelled to compose the epiphanies. My newest muses and revelations differed. The untapped themes came to fruition like another "aha" moment. New software for photo-collages was providing ideas for the themes as well. Given this unexpected crescendo, I began creating a prelude or backstory for the evolving chapters.

When I reread my *AHA* chapbook, I was humbled immediately. Over a decade later, I was gifted again. When, where, and how these new epiphanies burst onto PJ's scene became an unexpected pleasure. As a postscript, we writers savored these arousals and doted upon the brainstorming. I was no exception.

Given my educational wayfaring and degrees, a motivation for lifelong learning and a smattering of self-improvement, I was primed. Like other primed earthlings, I was hoping— to be on the brink of advanced perks of wisdom. It was still a time when we were "doing our thing" with our work, attending the diverse events, flying for our job endeavors or the pleasure trips, and enjoying the visits with endearing friends and family.

Personally, I had gravitated towards the dynamics of intention and manifestation. I was not alone. These refreshing beliefs were now prominent in our global world. People were still attending conferences and heading to retreats, never worried about the crowded venues.

I was part of these "now" moments. My Jitsu, Reiki-Shamballa certifications, and the metaphysical and meditative experiences with such talented professionals enhanced my mindfulness. There was a realm of "something special" to be tapped, given this esoteric world of uplifting dimensions, honor, and aptitude.

Legendary karma and pursuing a spirit-filled life were an open invitation for these like-minded individuals and a medley of professionals. Once again, I was making a conscious choice—respect and dignify my enlightenments. The "opportune timing" for all of us was about to be hindered.

I had almost finished this *Epiphanies* book. Then the horrific ordeals happened instantly. Our world turned upside-down with the daily, weekly, and monthly "breaking news." A global pandemic, ramped-up traumas that fleeted past the brink of surreal, and our "unknowns" appeared everywhere. Our technology, television, and compelling stories made "staying at home" and the "new normal" a reality of this ever-evolving world.

There was no absolute truth about our tomorrow. Our life, as many of us relived in hindsight, was put on hold. Within a few weeks, there was another hallmark. We were urged to be creative, explore an uncharted path, work remotely, and pursue the new ways to "stay connected" that were featured online.

The "stay at home" and "close to home" messages prompted many of us to take action and make alternative choices. The surreal and real perceptions were like a Richter scale on certain days or weeks. Beyond a shadow of a doubt, it became an understatement to say that finding our life-balance was priceless.

I made a fervent and valued choice. J continued this book, not knowing very much about tomorrow, let alone our future. If anything was to be a choice, it was my personal decision to forge ahead and make headway with my writing, amidst all of our escalating world scenarios.

I paused purposefully, took quality time to reflect and meditate, and watched the helpful YouTubes. I selected the videos that stressed how to strengthen our immunity and emotional well being. Oh my, I took less for granted—each day, every week, and across the months.

I opted to stretch for my personal quest of the daily, positive mindfulness, rather than the incessant angst and hopelessness. Endearing family and friends shifted to texts, emails, phone calls, and social distancing. My almost-complete book of epiphanies, re-awakenings, and our harmony was morphing. Would I reach its completion and eventual publication?

I did not know any more than the next earthling. No crystal ball? No magic fairy dust left on the grocery shelves. I was impassioned to keep moving forward in the direction of our mindfulness, the soul-filled experiences, and our optimism about the future.

Together. All of us needed to remain connected and stay tuned…

Respect of Alaska's pristine bounty, a soulful imprinting…
A panorama of the Danali National Park and the Inside Passage…
Glaciers, Dall mountain sheep, bull moose, and grizzly bears in their natural habitats…
Nature's glorious abundance, harvesting in our sublime consciousness…
The synchrony of Mother Earth Gaia—a treasure trove—with
our authentic appreciation of her preservation…

Our Legacy of Mother Nature

E ach of us makes a choice—daily, weekly, or monthly. To seize the giveaway moments and the gratuity that abound in Mother Nature is our choice. Perhaps, today is the day for a different decision?

Unforgettable moments in time trigger the new decisions. As I am finalizing this book, our world pandemic has catapulted us, beyond any carbon copy or semblance of our previous daily routines. Our lives feel at once, both real and surreal, given the compelling emotions. Staying at home, working remotely, experiencing the breaking news, taking precautions, and striving to make the next-best choices are the looming realities.

In my suburban condo and neighboring towns, people are still walking and running, with or without masks. Latex gloves or no gloves. Social distancing is respected. The required masks are now the postings on certain entry doors.

Different states issue the individual mandates. Neon tape is in use for stand-here positions, one-way aisles, and the entry versus exits at the grocery stores, pharmacies, post offices, and the banks.

I am not alone. People want to get outside for a respite, to take a deeper breath of fresh air, and soak up the Vitamin D in the sunshine. They want to catch glimpses of the budding-spring signatures of Mother Nature and snatch these moments for an appreciative reprieve or an inner solace.

For many of us, the phenomenal beauty and bounty of Mother Earth Gaia are an understatement. Quite simply, she bestows her beauty splendidly. She bequeaths her bounty—without expectation of any return or validation.

Mother Earth Gaia is quite capable of the ultimate ante up. Indeed, Mother Earth awes, bombshells, and presents us with the eye-openers and the lifetime lessons on any day, month, or year. Perhaps, given our present weeks of angst versus our reprieves and the connections, there is something else? We take less for granted.

Whatever the nature scenarios display, it is our chance to be hooked. Rapt attention optimizes the process of today's experiential learning. Nowadays, the renowned professionals offer timely and virtual videos.

Their gifts convey meaningful insights that upsurge or foster a memory lane. In the calm of Mother Nature, we often experience our flashbacks and a retrospection about the unconditional loves in our lifespan, present or past.

Several of us share. We relay the sanguine, positive signs from our significant others or loved ones after their death, especially when our heartfelt urgency or desire to commune arises.

These manifestations are often keepsakes—specific signs or traces in nature, as our significant others and loved ones cannot return as we knew them—the earthly human beings.

An unexpected butterfly in close proximity, a stunning bird mimicking our melody, a serendipitous dragon fly, an unforeseen cloud image, or a telekinetic wonder just arrive. Are we paying more heed to Mother Nature during the undulating tempo of our unprecedented crisis and the "new normal" days?

Remaining spellbound, engaged, and witnessing any of these signs and harbingers of compassion are no longer surreal. Many of us confide in one another and affirm each other's experience. We want to catch more of that charitable and awesome drift—an unequalled, inner peace.

Today? Tomorrow? All of us need to seek an intrinsic calm or peace to maintain our avenues of resilience and hope. All of us need a life-balance in the face of today's worries, angst, or the what-next fears. The legacy of Mother Nature often gifts us a tithe beyond measure and manifests that very essence of peace.

~~Remember leaving the toe-art messages or seashell insignia along an alluring ocean or lake shoreline? Entrust that a Mother-Nature intelligence is *still receiving* an earful of those good tidings and karma.

~~A dragon fly greets me on my patio. Candy-apple red or a gray-lavender, it comes to rest upon my hand, my forearm, or a foot. The tuned-in dragon fly cocks its tiny head, as I send today's heartfelt and ethereal messages to my loved ones.

~~Recapture and reminisce about the botanical joys that you felt when visiting a butterfly world. No desire to forget, reeling in the euphoria when a sensational butterfly landed upon you. Accept the summons. Did you become an "animal whisperer" in these mesmerizing moments?

~~Awaken and relive the magical and quintessential beauty of an enticing river. Canoe or kayak downstream. Be gifted with a willpower, a dauntlessness, the intrinsic desire, and a natural high. Paddle upstream. Now, close your eyes. Take pleasure in today's endless memories and those vibrant images of nature's gifts.

~~The Blue Ridge range of mountains enticed my stance upon stellar rocks to gaze afar. Honey bees were overshadowed. A morpho butterfly landed on my heart chakra, caressed my lips, and flew to a nearby lavender flower. This spirit of a loved one waited patiently to overhear my whispered, indebted messages. I still send my beholden messages…

~~Behold the hawks that soar in tandem. Feast your eyes upon their flight. Immerse yourself beneath the wings of cloud-angels. Today? Next week? Discern when this marvel will happen, this unexpected enhancement of sky art.

~~The beach sandcastles bequeath sugar-sand gemstones to June's full moon on our loggerhead turtle walk. A small group of us watched Mama lay upon a nesting scarp, dropping her precious eggs. In a month or two, her hatchlings would search for sunbeams cast upon the ocean, dodging every imaginable predator. My best friend, an Ohio Buckeye buddy, and I still chose to be grateful, look back, recount, and imagine once again…

~~Experience the natural high during today's walkabout. Relive your pursuits of the local, regional, national, or international globe-trotting. Your nomadic footprints created the thought-provoking passages with an awareness of the different textures. Enshroud in today's aromas, the sounds, the sunbeams, and a charismatic energy of Mother Nature. Savor the novel imagery and create the new memories during today's walkabout.

~~Rain mists in the forest transform into a stream of thirst-quenching sustenance. Tilt back slowly, sanction, and open your receptive, opening lips. Luxuriate in a purity like no other bestowal. Our weather still includes rainy days or rain droplets for our appreciative being. Open a door or a window. Go on a porch or deck with an umbrella. Take this reprieve, this quality time to refresh and re-connect.

~~Top off a favorite bucket with refreshing water. Add the passion fruits like the red apples, golden pears, and soft peaches. Go for the gusto—indoors or outdoors. Just do it! Take a dunk, submerge, and chomp into the fruitful goodness and glory of being.

~~Stroll to a nearby meadow or foot-path in the early evening. Sit on a softer blanket or stand in the stillness. Commune with the fireflies or close your eyes and call upon the remembrance. Let yourself feel like an awakened child again and again.

~~Danali Park and the "animal spirit" own an august, majestic terrain. Alaskan bull moose, caribou, grizzly bear mothers and cubs, wolves, and birds. Dall sheep dot the rocky ridges like tiny white puffery. All of their circadian rhythms and survival during the challenging seasons are beyond discernment. Honor—this call of the wild, who roam this daunting, breathtaking, and the protected land. How valuable is a memory bank of our travels, near or far, when those riches still evoke our tranquilizing calm?

~~Buy the simple sparklers that light up backyards, creating the festive neighborhoods. No special holiday or celebration. Just light up, wave energetically, and watch these glowing clusters through the eyes of your inner child. Have you erased or left behind these tempting, nostalgic memories of back yards and your extraordinary playtime?

~~Recall a hike to a pristine lakeside or ocean. Glorify the rhythmic pounding of the waves. Gaze at the moon. Breathe the cleansing air and exhale the daily stressors. Stay in nature's stillness. No worries of today, tomorrow, or the future encumber this authenticity of nature's peace. Mother Nature still awaits today's visit and our respectful reprieve.

~~The inherited beauty of nature is heralded. Are some of us forgetting or dismissing our lifetime connections? Can we elect to resolve today's challenges and be better caregivers in her preservation?

~~Look to your lineage, a family tree. How early did your ancestors begin to explore and value the beauty of nature? An agrarian society was not the sole reason to respect Mother Earth. Innate and intrinsic motivations to preserve and protect were ethical, first-class values. The legacy of preservation and protection awaits the new, front-line responders of our world—all of us.

~~The Inside Passage of Alaska is witnessed from charming ports like Juneau, Ketchikan, and Skagway. A foreshadowing is possible with smaller cruise ships. Rapid glacier recession is revamping the Inside Passage. Floating icebergs, appearing like crystal-Caribbean gemstones, already foretell the climatic cries and daily pleas. Tune in—to nature's hastening apocalypse. Envision and embrace a new timeline and our world unity for nature's turnarounds. Our attentiveness to the climate change is a mindful reconnection.

~~Our value of legacy and endowment is simple. Perhaps, a walkabout in the country or the green spaces that arouse our sensory pleasures. Perhaps, Mother Nature's unveiling of an unfurling or a saffron hibiscus flower. Perhaps, Mother Nature's emergence of the colorful tulips. Perhaps, Mother Nature's path of scented evergreens, reaching for the zenith of our breathtaking sky art. Simplify…

AWAY FROM
THE CITY

Magical carousel invites the PJ reprieve, soaring and drifting away from the city hype…
Another purposeful pause is a comical respite—my imagined splendor
of the exquisite lip-kissin' and cuddlin' on a bench…
A day for a fun-filled, looney shtick, near my witnesses—the vintage
lighthouse and smooth rocks, weathered by undulating waves…

Our Imagination and Flights of Fancy

Use your imagination. Be creative. How many times have any of us heard those phrases? Perhaps, we long for these creative nudges—back yonder and in our fast-changing world of work, at-home and online schooling, and the new government or state constraints. When, where, and how any of us may pursue our wanton travel, leisure time, and envisioned flights of fancy are ever-changing or still unknown.

I credit my parents for their unfaltering and timeless encouragements to be clever, ingenious, cool, or original with a PJ leading-edge vision. Today, as I was writing again, their parental impetus became a trigger, prompting me to look-back, relive, and recount the analogous reminiscences. I did. Here came the instantaneous flashbacks of my first grade teacher—the impressive Ms. C.

I was born in Ludlow, Massachusetts when it was an active mill town. A sense of "community" was the real deal, not a popular buzzword. Most of us walked to a small elementary school for the first grade. Nope—no Montessori, nursery, or preschools in this mill town.

Well, Ms. C. made her astronomic impacts. Our charming teacher had purple-gray hair and the biggest-ever teeth! Oh, wow—that unforgettable, linger perfume that we kiddos smelled all day long.

Dad watched me nibble a bit of my breakfast that morning. He smiled, praised me as "our big girl now," and topped off my special morning with a jumbo hug. I clasped Mom's hand tightly, as we strolled to school. Finally, we arrived. Both of us walked slowly into my sun-filled, cozy classroom.

Kids were already crying. Ms. C. was gently touching and bending over to give the children a pink kleenex. Mom paused, bent down, gave her butterfly-kiss, and winked lovingly at me.

Ms. C. was already beside me, smiling with her colossal teeth! Holding out a gargantuan hand, she offered, "Let's go to *your* desk!" I clasped her surprisingly soft hand, did a pretend-bravado walk to my chair, and touched the purple crayon on my desk. Every week, I liked the warmth in my tummy, whenever I gazed at my kindhearted teacher. Ms. C. floated 'round and 'round our vibrant classroom.

Ms. C. extended the alluring invitations. "Be creative. Use YOUR imagination!" She was always thrilled with everyone's story, art work, and our daily papers. Well, I just adored her. Something else was in the cards.

New schools! I had one female and two male teachers in my new elementary school, when my family made the move for my Dad's opportune job. Yikes, my middle sister and I were light-years behind in our subjects in our suburban schools near Boston, Massachusetts.

Most of my teachers were generous spirits, envisioning our unique ways of learning. They ramped up their inspirational vibes. I struggled and still stayed after school a lot. My parents helped with our homework, the teacher visitations, and our moving-forward goals.

The PJ mini-sobs happened in spite of the mutual efforts. My teachers owned a genuine compassion. A gentle cadence in their voices was reassuring and, eventually, restored the former PJ confidence and my flights of fancy.

Don't be afraid to be creative. Try to use your imagination. Why, I heard the same lingo at my new, challenging schools. Amazing! Shortly thereafter, I hustled out of the PJ self-sabotage box and sprinted—for my heartfelt passions. Even the gym teachers were enamored with the PJ fast-as-a-lightning-bolt running style and my dogged determination.

They declared that I needed to run with the guys on the playground, especially during our gym classes. My new girlfriends cheered me onward for years. Just imagine, this exposure of my running spirit—another PJ flight of fancy.

My junior and senior high schools revealed enough of the like-minded teachers. New friends and allies emerged like a beautiful dawn. My tribe…

I was not in the highest division and it took a long time to make the honor roll in high school. But, there was a valuable phenomenon in this new, suburban town—permission to be creative, think out-of-the-box, and keep stretching with a PJ verve.

I experimented with all of this gutsiness during my schooling adventures. By college, I was challenging certain professors—if-and-when their class climates and assignments were rule-bound, rigid, and incorporated no free-spirit reign.

Precocious child? Precocious adolescent? Precocious adult? Precocious was not being flippant, smart-alecky, or disrespectful. Lifetime lessons came to light. I learned to respect a diversity of learning styles and never forgot my best teachers.

The rest is history. I embraced that being "different or imaginative" was a five-star status. I chose to be immersed. Another meaningful flight of fancy came quickly. This acceptance of differences was fortuitous, especially in the public or private schools and during the decades of my collegiate and career experiences.

Little did I know… Little did any of us know…

These lifetime lessons of a recognition and an acceptance of our differences were fortuitous. These lifetime lessons were relevant for today's unity and our world countenance. They became invaluable for our daily efforts to believe, create, and sustain a life-balance. Ultimately, these lifetime lessons reaffirmed our togetherness and the evolving sanctions for our global world.

~~Rise up. Meet any challenges with a loving-kind demeanor and a gentle disposition. Go forward with this unencumbered attitude. Skyrocket—as much as possible. Yesterday, today, tomorrow, or even next month? Applaud—all of our encores to skyrocket together.

~~Impeach the persistent road blocks and detours. Never doubt, dread, or forget the rise-above belief and those sentiments. A positive mindset increases our altitude with daily living and our experiences.

~~Chase after a flight of fancy. Do what excites or inspires you. Infuse tomorrow, next week, and another year with these forthcoming flights of fancy. Accept that this ascending phenomenon is still a part of today's journey. One or several years ago? None of us knew. Today? None of us knows—exactly when and where our flights of fancy, the lifetime lessons, and our journey will change.

~~Just imagine… Transform into a mermaid at the Isle of Capri on the breathtaking Amalfi coast. Fantail through the "Eternal Tunnel of Love." Acknowledge that today's imagination and transformation are not merely a destination, but provide us with an unconditional peace of being.

~~A professor encouraged our creative projects in lieu of a run-of-the-mill endeavor. Surges of excitement, until my B minus grade. He touted my creative talents, but… I *deserved* my B minus grade? Classmates did not pursue the creative projects, so my grade was lowered—his class curve. We talked and he stated, "I'll give you a B instead." At 19, I repeated his class encouragements, valuing of my creative talents, and something else. "You did not *give* me that B minus to B grade. I *earned* even a higher grade. Just for the record? I believed your class invitation." As I stood up, my professor expressed his respect—PJ's spunk and creative talents. I gave a wassup-stare and departed, realizing that the value of self-worth and my energy reserves were fundamentally my choice. Lifetime lessons appear at any age.

~~Imagine the intense hues of a picturesque fall foliage. Let this chromatic and royal season become a trust fund. Each passing year, pause to receive an unveiling of these intangible riches—a lifetime of gift-giving. Welcome, the 2020 fall foliage when it begins to unveil the wealth that enhances your trust fund.

~~Let any gala celebration, deserving of front-page news, spur a flight of fancy. Imagine another bold headliner, honoring your *Birth*day. FaceTime, social media, or drive-by well wishers that keep the social distance still matter. Car horns, hoots and hollers, balloons, and their festive posters. Let whatever frolic, gaiety, and wingding-jubilee linger—as a memorable, progressive party. Glorify that a distinctive enerCHI—YOU presented to our world on your special day—was no mistake.

~~Partake of a myriad of flights of fancy. Do not stop dreaming for a future. Hobbies, interludes of quiet, visits with significant others, travels, and fulfilling experiences are not forbidden novelties in our dreamscapes. Go ahead and instigate these flights of fancy. Be mindful. Set free an imaginative spirit—for yourself and our world with positive manifestations.

~~Off the cuff. Flights of fancy that are imagined, but not yet pursued and savored? Just do it— brainstorm a multitude of these envisioned flights of fancy. Imagination costs nothing, always gratis. 'Tis an underrated freebie...

~~IMAGINATION. Check out the capitalized word on this page. If this visual sighting creates a warm, familiar buzz or intensifies an authentic boost, just keep on truckin'. No guilt or regrets. Imagination serves us well during catastrophic events, an impasse in our life, or the dire straits of a crisis. Keep making IMAGINATION a must-do milestone, a passionate pursuit, and the daily stimulation for a life-balance. Why not?

~~Dreams. Free-flowing thoughts, our meditations, and the musings throughout our day and the weeks. Each grouping can become substantial, sharpened, and befitting. Planning often includes a part of our daydreams. Keep planning—try adding an individual zest of artistry, fantasy, and a vivid creation.

~~Flights of fancy may not be in your current repertoire of phrases. This phrase may not be remembered. It may be on the back burner. Never say never. Act upon one flight of fancy. Try a second flight of fancy? Attitude = Altitude. I wrote that subtitle over 6 years ago and it still resonates in today's world...

~~Trigger a sense of well being. Recollect the characteristic moments during childhood, adolescence, or adulthood that were fancied. Oversee, shepherd, and usher in a potential for the additional array of fanciful moments. Use this attentive and escorting spirit on any day or week, as our stay-at-home efforts continue.

~~Conjecture. Fantasize. Guess. Picture. Dream up. Make up. Trail blaze. Just go for it—with each of the esteemed flights of fancy. Grandiose or small efforts still matter. Enterprising efforts during our pandemic keep bringing forth the new brainstorming, the hopeful outcomes, and a better potential for our resolutions.

~~Risk-taking is one highway that leads to imagination. Do not exit too soon. Forego the breakdown and fast lanes. Just tempt fortune or fate to discover a new boulevard. Enjoy the right of way, leading ASAP to your imagination.

~~Free will is our choice. The opportune moments to keep going forward with an imaginative spirit abound. Be mindful. Today? Tomorrow? Get hooked on becoming *more* mindful.

~~Each of us is capable of exercising our right of ownership. The proprietary rights of gratitude are waiting for our vote. A quintessential essence of gratitude may remain illusive, but not impossible or improbable in today's world.

~~Originality, ingenuity, vision, innate desires, and an enterprising spirit are meaningful facets of gratitude. We are quite capable of inquiring and probing at different life stages. Compelling stories on our global news are a precious affirmation. All of us are gifted.

~~What do you fancy? Leave no stone unturned. Look into possibility, regardless of our world scenarios. Turn resourcefulness, ingenuity, and fantasy inside out. Dig into their depths. This process of discovery learning is limitless. Do not forget or abandon the unconditional love and care of you...

UNCONDITIONAL LOVE...

Not mere words, redundancy, or expressed trivia...
Rare moments of the "now" and unvarnished truth-seeking...
Create quality time to connect and explore our togetherness...

Free Spirits and Our Synchrony

When we least expect or envision, another free spirit breezes into our life. Happenstance or meant to be? Many of us dwell upon, revive, and hold dear the dialogues, the immediate rapport, and the mutual intrigue.

There is a sense that a melding of pathways occurs for a special reason, which may or may not be crystal clear at that moment. One inference, given an intuition and our lifetime lessons, becomes apparent and greeted with a personal vitality and curiosity.

An existing or new kindred-spirit connection is heartening. A chance meeting of a like-minded individual supports a significant affirmation. A human desire for the unconditional caring, a spontaneity, and our mutual traits in a fast-paced and self-absorbed world are still authentic. Nowadays, our day-to-day world is transforming how each of us maintains a meaningful connection.

When there is an obvious, synchronistic balance between us, something else crops up rather naturally. Mutual enlightenments and the charismatic appeals still happen. Both of us still seek an investment of quality time and mutual efforts, even with our worldly constraints.

How do two "free spirits" keep up with a capricious meeting and an unforeseeable momentum of a different world? Online? Texting? Social media? Visits outdoors with social distancing? Or just go with the flow—in our uncertain and erratic world?

If each individual makes a commitment, certain attributes become the actual foreshadowing. Trust, the risk-taking, and an obvious courage permit our crisscrossing paths to evolve, creating an admirable countenance.

The natural ebb-and-flow are legitimate indications. The non-judgements, the leaps of conviction, and a common cultivation open our doors. Figuring out the ways to stay connected in an ever-changing world are definite challenges and the ongoing realities.

Whenever this synchronistic phenomenon transpires, a bona fide attachment persists—as the rousing emotions and a dynamic gift. Why now—this time and this place in our life wayfaring along with our world still turning upside-down? Yet, the humanness—our courage and hope—still surface.

Does either person really own a choice, given the mutual feelings? Hmm, what angelic guides or celestial guardians put the auspicious cards on the table? What ethereal guides put forth the plans for this chance and significant meeting?

Certain realizations come to light. Both individuals cherish a free-spirit nature and a bravado throughout life stages. Free will, a boldness, and the viable options still matter, regardless of what is transpiring in our uncertain, erratic, and tenuous world. Slivers of hope and optimism remain the beacons of light.

Each individual dares to commit—to the virtuous leaps of courage, to share, and to find the ways to sustain the connection, given our global pandemic and the circumstances. Time always reveals the humble realms—of living *and* giving in a frenzied, chaotic world.

Amazing grace arrives in spite of any local, regional, or world scenarios. There is no price tag with a bestowal and this uncommon bounty during our "new normal" or any challenging times in our lifespan.

Our "remotely connected" world and social changes make our challenges appear and reappear. With long-term kindred spirits, there is little social distancing. Behold the hand-holding, a close proximity, and the caring as the real signs.

With kindred spirits who start a new connection, there is a certain amount of re-awakening. We still experience an array of our human emotions. There is still the desire for quality time. We decide to capture a reserved space, the energy, and our hopeful and faithful pursuits, in spite of the impending life scenarios in our evolving and complex world.

~~Walk along a pathway, holding hands with your significant other. Leave behind the incessant chatter of the ego mania and any of the judgments. Release and entrust that a free spirit reign will come forth again.

~~The heart's desire. Intention. Passion. Free will. Free choice. How long do we want to neglect, dismiss, or tune out what is still possible?

~~Our egos adore the chit-chatter. Overwhelmed? Take three deep breaths. Calm the nerves. Savor the beginning infusion of endorphins, a pleasurable elixir and an unfailing chemical release. Synchronize the heart and willingness to find the depths of an inner peace and our unity.

~~Silent vows of partners, caressing Mother Earth Gaia and cosmic life forces, transmute an intuitive knowing. Synchronistic impulses awaken, leaving an indelible imprinting upon the mind, body, and the spirit of each individual. Never lose sight of the gift of giving.

~~Intertwined, a gentle cadence of breaths. Lovers transform during the night vigil with their dreamscapes. Their sleep-entrustment evolves into an unexpected bestowal and an inheritance. Let the inheritance continue…

~~Summon today's intention to witness again. Recapture the memories. Go to a dance venue. Watch for the songs, tempo, and a cadence that create a vibration between the synchronistic partners. Witness how their blissful aura refreshes, breathes new life, and replenishes the energy field. Today or tomorrow? Listen to the music and dance—indoors or outdoors. Re-awaken your authentic dance spirit.

~~ Ascending souls—one in another—is rare. So partake of the breath work, daily meditations, and enter a light-filled kaleidoscope of chakra energies that ease our mourning. Our loss of adored human beings whose last earthly moments were not in our presence? Explore today's meditations and acceptance with another chance of a loving reunion with those ascending souls, and now, our guardian messengers.

~~State-of-the-art transforms into a space for an openness and the shifting gears in our day or week. Where does that risk-taking and the dauntless re-connections chart our course on that particular day or week?

~~There is a confusion or the miscommunication. Our eyes witness this moment of naked personas and the esteemed human qualities. The courage to dialogue becomes a liberation, a gift, and a legacy for our perennial togetherness.

~~Nonconformists respect a free-spirit realm. Learning is a process not a "quick fix" state of mind. Our "new normal" is a daily reminder. We endeavor to become more mindful, flexible, and resilient. Lifelong learning and the new, forthcoming self-improvements become the respectful principles and our ultimate ideals.

~~Simpatico partners release any of the melodramas. Bonding is a genuine heirloom rather than a thespian art of stagecraft or the superimposed and egocentric roles.

~~Ceaseless moments to own an attitude of gratitude with a significant other are present and undeniable at any age. Watch the partners of longevity that never lost their steadfast sparks of a thankful attitude. Their ingenuity and an admirable flair remain a beloved work-in-progress.

~~Souls in tandem maintain a distinct individuality. The testimonials and their humanitarian acts of unconditional giving and receiving are not platitudes. Even our "breaking news" includes and honors these partners.

~~Partners unite. There are years of connectivity and appreciation. One partner leaves our earthly plane. The other partner is healthy, but ascends shortly thereafter. Their soulful and devoted connections? Their cosmic forces of eternal love? No medical reasons or explanations are germane.

~~A compelling troupe of like-minded people are irresistible. Any of us can learn and gain from our differences and similarity, whenever we recognize and accept these opportunities. The commercials on television show the exponential growth of certain companies, the communities, and diverse people extending their generosity of monies and an encouraging spirit. This togetherness for our future is sustaining the ultimate unity.

~~A potential legacy in-the-making happens. Across generations, the partners make a conscious choice to love unconditionally. Is it easier to say than do? Is it easier to give up with any arduous or the wearisome weeks or years? Free spirit empowers our free will and the choices. What is the free will and a choice in your partnership?

~~What is togetherness? A life force of souls in sync or harmony? Do not let any arbitrary or unreasonable societal influences define a personal reality or a decisive moment, day, or year. Do not give up or overlook the energy, a durability, and the countenance imbedded in a genuine togetherness. Our daily news includes the touching and affirmative features of this togetherness, even during the unpredictable times and our worldly constraints. The authenticity is not ignored or ever doubted...

Dreamscapes of yesterday and today hold a promise…
Stretch for the daily sustenance and a spirit of knowing…
Own a chutzpah with the pipe dreams and daily manifestations
of the ardent hopes and a visionary outlook…

Our Dreamscapes and Pipe Dreams

There are books on dreams that enliven and energize us. Our dreams are often symbolic or compelling, adding to our wisdom. If we awaken from a dream, there is an opportunity for the good fortune. A journal on a nightstand near the bed is one way to keep our dream-connections alive.

Many of us discover that we cannot flash back to a specific part or even the entirety of our dreamscape. Perhaps, we do not remember a dream, as it is symbolic of our pandemic and the unknown future? Perhaps, another dream is a keepsake because of a good night's rest? So, a few scribbles in a journal become the in-demand links to today's relevancy and new enlightenments.

Unquestionably, it is not easy to be semi-awake and journal. Our snoozing in La-La land outshines the journaling thang! Yet, the baby steps with cryptic notes or a unique shorthand create a stronger likelihood that we reclaim a higher quality of that particular dreamscape.

In hindsight, our dreams often represent the fleeting fragments, a forgotten memoir. At least we own a fair shake and better prospects with our journaling aspiration, the initiatives, and an enterprising energy.

All of us own a fighting chance and those nuggets of good fortune, whenever we make an effort to record, scrawl, or doodle the essence of a specific dream. Jotting down an anecdote or the imagery, whether technicolor or black and white, permits our brain synapses to give birth. Birth? Indeed, we begin to fabricate the sharpened and sophisticated connections.

We awaken to greet a memorable day or an unexpected week with the emergence of these self-actualized insights. Rise and shine does not seem to be such a cliche or triviality. Why not give our "journaling thang" a whirl or our best shot whenever the "best timing" occurs?

Nothing to lose with our deliberate efforts. The gratuity of knowing morphs into a part of our life chronicles. If we elect to save these mini-journals of personal dreams, just imagine our stockpile? Becoming a hoarder—a healthy miser—of these dreamscapes brings forth a healthier pathway to our first-class insights and deserving edification.

Losses? Grief and mourning? Worries? Our daily world in flux and a potential resolution or ideas for our loved ones? Throughout troubled times, several of us forget. Our memory loss is unintentional, but we forget about our valuable dreams and hopeful pipe dreams.

We still deserve the pleasure and joys in our life. A re-awakening of a better attitude and a higher altitude serves us well in the risky, the unsettling, and even, the unresolved times.

~~Lay down and rest. Choose the comfy pillows. Enfold into an essence of relaxation, a catnap or forty winks, and the slumberland. Entrust that a siesta extracts the best from the mastermind, our phenomenal brain. Dreamscapes are often a comfort, a diversion, or the palliative rest—to release any nonstop or relentless thinking about yesterday, today, and the future.

~~Request technicolor dreams before going to a beloved Shangri-la, a deep slumber, or catching the wanton shut-eye. Let the larger-than-life pipe dreams beget an imaginative journal. Discover this extra special treasure of scripting any part of a dreamscape. Our written words are rarely forgotten or ousted.

~~Dreams that inform and uplift us are stunning, unorthodox, and even electrifying. Our brain hemispheres, like Einstein and Einsteinette, present each of us with the smashing pipe dreams. Paradise found, not lost. Visions abound with the astonishing images and our stories of potential and possibility. Today's world is still befriended with the potential and possibility—our humanitarian efforts and the steadfast connections.

~~Our intuition is a healthy and ingenious daydream unfolding. No castaways or any harsh judgments are necessary. An acceptance of the prosperity is a manifestation of our higher self.

~~Just pop the question. Ask to dream—before falling into the REM and that slow-wave slumber. Our unremitting languor produces an inner calm, often in the grandiose company of our affirmations and a covenant for our vital replenishment.

~~Technicolor and vibrant dreams manifest our preeminent gifts. They are impressive reminders. They are striking remembrances. Begin a journal with this goodness and your joy. Divulge the surge of positive feelings. Rereading any passage honors your dignity and the virtues of a positive memory lane. Positiveness begets positiveness.

~~Forgetting or dismissing our pipe dreams happens. Practice the art of jotting down and saving the anecdotes. Our steady practice matters. This intention begins to identify any of the leftover angst, our subliminal hopes, and the pipe dreams for our quests and the coveted future.

~~Intertwine with a significant other. Curl up. Snuggle. Cuddle. Share affections. Honor the dual-release of the endorphins. Drift yonder…in a mystical dreamscape of togetherness.

~~No detours with today's breaking news or bothersome, foreboding television programs. Choose comforting music, a meditation, an engaging hobby, or a nature stroll or hike. Let go of today's drama. Experience an inspirational world of pipe dreams during these gratifying and palliative moments of relaxation.

~~Daydream about travel—local, regional, or international. Let the "heartbeat" of a favorite state, city, or village enter the day. Acting upon the option to daydream downloads into our heart—as the intangible wealth across our lifetime.

~~Wake up—from an illustrious, pleasurable daydream. Appreciate the heightened consciousness from this relaxed musing. Appreciate that being "in-the-zone" accentuates our positive energy vibrations as well.

~~Dream of the string vibrations in our elegant universe. Imagine the subtle and resonant waves. String vibrations connect the like-minded people. Become more mindful of these truths. Then choose to adopt and accept the art of attentiveness throughout the day, week, or month.

~~Intentional intermissions, the siestas, and our free-fall into an abyss of peace are tithes or giveaways beyond measure. The personal prerogative to defuse our stressors on each day, a week, or the month is as powerful as the forty-winks slumberland. Intentional intermissions are a humane and kindhearted reprieve during any of our rise-above days.

~~Pipe dreams are not forbidden. Societal or familial messages tend to pooh-pooh the power of imagination that resides in our pipe dreams. Are you daydreaming again? Your idea is crazy, not going to happen in your lifetime. Does this question or declaration sound familiar? Continue to vote "yes" to our pipe dreams that are supposedly out-of-bounds, taboo, or vetoed.

~~How do certain words or declarations become more "weighty" than others? Forget such a pursuit—dreams are a *waste* of time. Do not expend any energy and time on a pipe dream, especially in today's world. When and how did these negative judgments stop us in our tracks? No pauses or any reconsiderations? We elected not to pursue a dream, a pipe dream, or heaven forbid, go forward with our envisioned pursuits.

~~Permit "plenty of rope," just like the cliche. Adopt a laissez-faire attitude about any of the impending judgments. Indulgence and a free spirit come with experiencing our positive realms of being and becoming. Maintain the elbowroom for an unrestricted space of joy and the self-love. Favor this special intention as a top notch priority, a deep-rooted purpose of fine merit—for our worldly connections *and* your soulful being.

~~Be savvy. Adopt a creative genius and the chutzpah. Be astute enough to capture and hang onto a pipe dream, no matter what is happening in life. Seize the day, permitting a pipe dream to come to fruition. When pipe dreams lead to unraveling solutions—for us and our world—we call it "genius."

~~Hold fast to your dreams, as though each of them are high profile and very meaningful to your life's mission. Relive these dreamscapes. Snatch the bait. Remain hooked. Strive for the "dreamcatcher" of your day or week.

Intentions of self-actualized possibility and potential…
My life-force manifestations, beholden and gratifying…
My "Solstice" drumming circle, welcoming the re-awakenings…
Honorable greetings to the future—our hopes, passionate
renewals, and an elixir of golden abundance…

Our Intentions and Manifestations

Our intentions in the "now" or the present moment are fascinating. From these collectible minutes or occasions, there is a natural mindset to extract our daily manifestations. We still remain quite capable of creating the experiences about what to discern, earmark, contemplate, and foresee.

There is a stronger acceptance in our present world. We are old, wise souls at different ages and stages of life, as evidenced by our "breaking news" stories. This intrinsic desire is evolving with our toughest times—to learn the practice and art of intention. With the potential manifestations come the healthier, blossoming perks for different generations—to dote upon a new appreciation, a modern aptitude for solutions, and a state-of-the-art gratitude.

Today's metaphysical realms are overstocked with these abundant intentions and manifestations of different dimensions. YouTubes, social media connections, and our virtual outreach are available in today's world of catapulting statistics and the ever-changing forecasts. No question as to why the spiritual, transformative, and metaphysical realms remain teeming and replete.

The depths of spirituality are chockablock and jam-packed with relevant images and generous messages for seeking an inner calm on a daily basis. There are plentiful insights and diverse explorations for each of us. Namaste!

It is really no surprise as to why today's psychic mediums, the reiki and jitsu masters, the medical intuitives, and our spirit-filled professionals are appearing on a regular basis. Valued television features, international and national connections, and online-speaking engagements are given credence and respect in our fast-paced, mind-boggling world. Not too long ago, cruise excursions even offered a medley of metaphysical professionals for interested patrons, as an enticing part of their travel excursions and ports of call.

Today's world, it is a-changin' and evolving at a warp-speed, far beyond the mid-1960s and that wanton, wayfaring pop culture. Today's realities are equally dynamic, but typified as chaotic, too frenzied, and full of the unpredictable anxieties or an angst.

Truths be known, nothing in our world is static. There are fewer denials. Today's helter-skelter nature exposes our disconcerting environments, abounding with the daily "breaking news" on a local, regional, and global matrix.

We witness the realism in concert with such overstimulation. Many of us admit to feeling overwhelmed, depressed, apprehensive, or still fearful. Perhaps, a specific day or week presents an opportune or the essential and quality time to pause longer. Contemplation and discovery learning become the viable options for a personal rejuvenation and our urgency for a life-balance.

What else does each of us manifest? Take our purposeful breaks, meditate to release any self-created or worldly stressors, and aspire to illuminate the novel pathways. We want to possess more peace of mind and a heightened degree of calmness. There is definitely a tad bit more of our humane composure with these meaningful, accessible revelations in the "now."

All of us deserve harmony rather than the contrived blues, a daily disquiet, or the perpetual worries and the angst. Acceptance of our harmonic connections resonate with an active mindfulness and our human quests for the fresh beginnings.

These avid and passionate pursuits bring a wanton and cultivated "stillness" to each of us. This human "stillness" permits the hope, an optimism, and our humanitarian efforts to remain at the forefront of our daily living.

~~Intentions happen in the "now." To seize these opportune minutes or seconds is gratifying. Interconnected manifestations begin to amplify. Together, we step-up the process of regenerating and bolstering our soul-filled being.

~~A childhood of naked truths, being free of a myriad of inhibitions. An adolescence of authenticity, being able to pursue the preferred rites of passage. An adulthood of few abandonments, being able to savor the ultimate keepsakes. Envisioning this lifetime of flourishing development and self-esteem—for ourselves and humankind—is a solid intention and manifestation.

~~Create an endowment entitled, "Intentions and Manifestations for Humanity." Contribute to its net worth each day, week, or month. These intangible riches that accompany more compassion far exceed any other kind of endowment.

~~Witness the imagery in our imperial sky hues and the impressive clouds. Gaze upward, higher into an imagined apex. No abyss—as you choose to journey from your root-to-crown chakras into a higher dimension. Know that your loved ones are the manifestations of a guardian watch over humanity.

~~Ponder a positive phrase or thought. Bring forth a confident intention for that thought to rise to a healthier indulgence. The power of our human will and disclosures is no longer a secret or an illusion.

~~As a Reiki-Shamballa master, there is always a communication of positive intentions for my deserving clients. Their respect for my resonant vibrations and genuine manifestations is in sync, mystical, and fine-tuned. Together, we connect.

~~Release a personal intention to have a full-fledged, grandiose day. At the bong of midnight, it is a rarity to be disillusioned about today. It feels superlative not to feel upset, disappointed, or in a miserable funk. Try your superlative release...

~~Sudden chills, a tingling, a welling of tears, an image in the clouds, or the signs in nature. These clues crop up and recur with my reiki or whenever I take a hiatus, a breathing spell, and begin to wonder. Just ask...

~~A piggy bank becomes symbolic. Save a penny, a nickel, a dime, or a quarter on a daily basis. Make a resolution to build a trust fund. This trust fund continues to manifest a commitment, the solid verdict of our esteemed ownership and those gifts. Today, I chose the relief funds and a longtime donation. Loving kindness came full circle.

~~Intention is a cultivated form of expression. Being forthright and kind allows the value or worth of that expression to come forth. Believe that a radiance of light with a humane self-expression evolves. We receive exactly what we intend.

~~How does the "now" present itself in our ramped-up world? Take a purposeful break. Find a peaceful spot. Pause, slow down to stop the mind chatter, and concentrate on a deeper breathing. In those particular moments called the "now," the quietness or stillness arrives. Practice and partake. There is no confusion with this exquisite time capsule of gentle repose.

~~Intention and mindful immersion are purposeful. A positive manifestation is the result of that energy vibration and a life force. Our free spirit embodies this daily choice and the positive energy that flows into our world.

~~Say "no" to the chaotic pace of any irksome or nerve-racking day. Declare an adamant "yes" to an alternative pace change from today's world scenarios. Be humble, patient, unassuming, and non-resistant. Accept that the better life innovations are in-the-works.

~~A positive mindset and intentional catalysts are not correlated with a quick-fix mentality. A work-in-progress "mindfulness" and an energetic flow exemplify our beacons—of risk-taking and our self-worth. Moving forward in the seasons of our life is a tonic for the restorative-cellular connections. Together, there is a unique power in moving forward...

~~There are untrodden or virgin footpaths on any life journey. When and why do we take a less travelled boulevard? The mediocre, predictable passages of our past become a default. The uncontaminated and unseasoned walkways represent a brighter potential for our wholehearted re-awakening and the recharging.

~~Boredom is an intention. Exploration is an intention. Whatever choice that we pursue, there are inevitable outcomes or the sequels. The complexion of our intention begets a quality—a can of worms or the potential for the better spin-offs?

~~The potpourri of moments—from the cradle to our death—are certainties. Purposeful recollections of the positive imprints and magnetism reveal a difference in our attitude and the altitude. Our lofty mindset and elevated summit soar quite nicely, as a manifested unveiling and epiphany. Let our world remain mindful.

~~Life force is an energy. Spur or repel? Boost or constraint? Motivate or denigrate? Encourage or malign? Life force creates or dismisses our developing and reformist humanity.

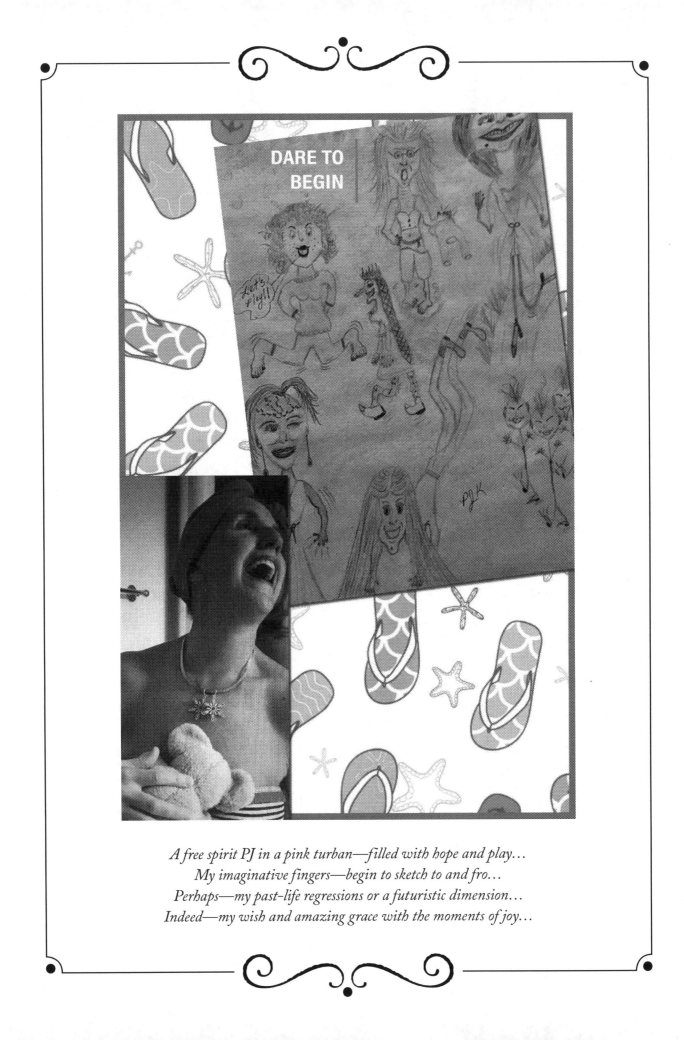

A free spirit PJ in a pink turban—filled with hope and play…
My imaginative fingers—begin to sketch to and fro…
Perhaps—my past-life regressions or a futuristic dimension…
Indeed—my wish and amazing grace with the moments of joy…

To Be or Not to Be? Our Playtime

Act like an adult. Behave yourself. Be the perfected, or at least, the cultured and sophisticated grown-up. The reprimands, like an overplayed recording or melodrama, are relentless. So are the instantaneous embarrassments of those individuals who make minimal allowances for comic relief. They do not condone our playtime throughout adulthood. Perhaps, there is more acceptance?

Bombarded. Overwhelmed. We are at an obvious time—regionally, nationally, and internationally—where more adults yearn for the comic relief. They are trying to alleviate personal and worldly stressors that surround our pandemic.

Television spots with comedians at home, the funny sitcoms, and the replays of former comedians help us to defuse and release the stress. These whimsical replays and the new virtual venues are opening the beneficial doors for our emotional well being and a better life-balance.

Our desires and playful actions—about the months-ago when everything was not upside-down? Null and void, especially from the individuals with those reprimands to act like an adult. No reasons for our adult playtime. For shame. Before today's adoption of this shameful stigma, it is high time to underscore the credible research about amusement and our pleasures.

Amusement, play, and our sense of humor reduce the negative stressors. The physiological self actually feels the vibrations of our laughter and chuckles. The psychological self appreciates the slow-mo pace and relaxing, silly spirit in our daily living.

This lighthearted orientation counteracts the constant undulations, turmoils, or realities of a burdensome day or week in today's world. Our hassles, the moodiness, the squabbles, or most struggles come into a better perspective or lessen, whenever our sense of humor or playtime arrive on the scene.

Spring's arrival brings another sighting for playtime. I love to watch the children ride their bikes, run around the lawns or walkways, and try to keep an obvious foreign rule of "social distancing" during their playtime. Their parents and allies are smiling. In fact, the parents are more playful than ever.

The parental insights are affirmative. There is still optimism, value, and an enthusiasm about a "brighter side" to living our life. Other adults make conscious choices to take advantage of the jogging, a power-walk, a meditation, different styles of yoga, fun hobbies, or other diverting options to promote an enriched attitude and well being.

Strong-willed adults are not procrastinating or waiting too long to play with their kids or grandkids. They are not self-critical or overly worried. Their decision to experience the upgraded joys in their present life ventures is still a beneficial and rewarding exploration.

Go for our gusto—to experience the enjoyments, the euphoria, the chuckles, and super stress alleviators. Why not? No one owns a crystal ball. Well, I have not met or heard of anyone that has spotted that crystal ball. Nor do I know anybody who is tight with the fairy godmother that grants all wishes.

Time means the "now" and in the next nanosecond, endearing earthlings. There are no guarantees regarding today, even the minutes and hours ahead of us. Our conscious choices of how to live, how to play, and any meaningful questions regarding when-and-where are pertinent to our well being.

It is never too late to "go for the gusto" with our amusements, a sense of humor, and a precious spirit of playtime. Our "breaking news" and daily stories are real, not to be forgotten or dismissed. A temporary, on-hold pattern and our impassioned choice to pause for the laughter, our delights, and the playtime are too valuable to forsake.

~~We nestle harder into the soft pillows, thinking that our peals of laughter will be muffled. Not possible! Our innermost child usurps the older adult, lest we almost forget.

~~Enjoy the prolonged laughter. Our tummy hurts so good. Chuckles and belly laughs arrive, if a search-and-find mission is adopted voluntarily. A sophisticated, quick-witted, and worldly-wise intelligence bobs up and drops its anchor. We are being liberated and redeemed in the nick of time.

~~Do not pretend, endorse, or assume that human beings should always act like the serious adults. Children and teens are getting a sneak preview of us. In good times or during the hardships in life? They are still learning and soaking up—our sagacious wit, charismatic joys, and a commitment to maintain a sense of humor and our much-needed playtime.

~~Play makes us earthlings more humane, less illusive. Let a radiant lightheartedness and the unconditional caring touch all of humankind.

~~Cast the die. Treasure the daily opportunities for our beguiling pleasures. Whoopee! Grins and a contentment signal a resonance with our delighted soul and the catchy "oh-ah" moments. In the days and weeks of drastic predictions, all of us need at least a few "oh-ah" moments.

~~Let 'em rip—the outrageous and unhinged belly laughs. No regrets. Know that the instant rejuvenation and unforgettable bliss have arrived—right on cue.

~~Raise the bar for "wicked good" fun and whimsy. Embrace the philosophy that the adult buffoonery, the shenanigans, and a frolic are the A-1 and spectacular infusion. Yes, glorious infusions! Our mind, body, and spirit actually groove with these natural endorphins.

~~Peals of laughter and laugh-snorts await our intentional kick-start. Appreciative living is simple. Remember that intentional kick-start on a certain day? EnJOY…

~~Send a purposeful blast of cheerio straight to your heart. Dispatch another lavish blast. Choose to make a difference in the quality of a dis-heartening day.

~~Raise the "tee-heeing" and wondrous "laugh-snorting" to an exotic art. Know that our giggle meters are ascending to an exponential height. Today, tomorrow, or next week? Do not abandon a human longing to laugh, even though there are certain days for the compassion and our empathic tears.

~~Acting loosey goosey and kickin' up our heels are the best-ever brouhaha. Thumbs up to these precious moments—the inestimable seconds of hullabaloo and livin' large. Surrender to a few precious moments…

~~Text a laugh-firmation to a person who needs a few chuckles. Envision the amusement, the har-de-har, and a text coming full circle in your time of need.

~~Pay forward the free goodies that crop up in our life. Pay forward is an unwavering and willful action, not a mere cliche.

~~Jolly Mon reigns supremo with our mind, body, and soul. The vital sparks, a life force, a dauntlessness, and our earnestness prevail. Cheerio with our efforts…

~~The yuck-it-up motto makes more friends than enemies. Try a bit of the engaging amusement. Make the sociable connection rather than missing an opportune moment.

~~Do not ignore or postpone a fire in the belly. No rain check or putting the super tummy aches on hold. Let our bonfire of the tummy rip with the utmost fanfare and a stupendous ruckus. Gloat and luxuriate in the aftermath of this luminous inferno. Choose to relive the luxury of such memories on any day or week.

~~Snicker, snort, chortle, crack up, and dare to howl like a coyote in a forested meadow. Howl again without any of the self-judgments. Experience the immediate boosts and shift in loftiness. Take a few moments to search and find another reason to snicker or laugh. Our mind, body, and spirit are waiting…

~~Witness the crazed havoc in our world during any week. Breaking news! Strive for an untapped, stellar point of view and a positive demeanor. Our undertaking and our committal are rarely a whoops or bad idea.

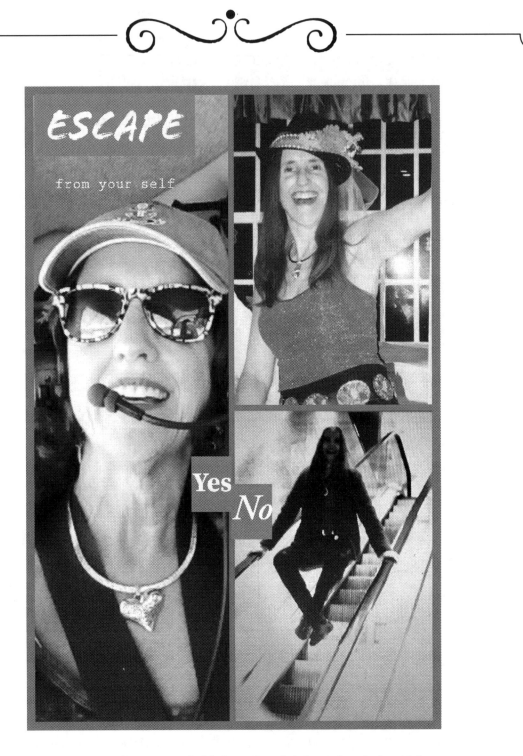

ESCAPE

from your self

Yes
No

*A life force of my inner-child abounds, a heightened and plentiful
essence of forthcoming ways to be creative...*
*This energy befriends my earthly soul with spontaneity and fewer
inhibitions, regardless of my young-elder stage of life...*
*These quintessential nudges come from a richer realm of
younger and the side-tracked endowments...*
This energy-force becomes an invitation, helping me to create my new lifetime journey...

Our Dares and Grabbers

Little kiddos love to dare, spoof, and razz one another. A lack of inhibition permits them to grab for the zeal in a heartbeat. Yesterday? Maybe tomorrow? When do we recollect seeing or hearing an abundance of adults offer an identical invitation to their friends or family?

When does this phenomenon of "daring" become too spooky for us grown-ups? Or unconventional? Not in vogue—especially at our mature ages? More than ever, many of us express that we are truly missing a part of our daring spirit. Or our fun dares with like-minded friends. Global precautions and safeguards are vital, but giving up completely on our zest and chutzpah is not mandatory.

Do we actually prolong a much-earlier societal realm of not stepping over that *invisible line*? No risks and no dares to trespass?

If we really care about our chutzpah, why not try to extend an empathic dare that was put on-hold for too long? A phone call or a "social distance" walk and talk. We dare a best friend to stop smoking. Tough love and stop smoking during a world pandemic? Yah, right now is actually the most precious time to commune and dialogue about what matters in life. Aim for "living large" and much longer.

Be sure to make that loving-kind pact to live until ripe ole' ages. Together, both of you envision the next dares of seizing such fun together. Do not forget to manifest—until 80 or 90 years young-at-heart. Playtime together becomes that must-do with one another. Please celebrate that these playful dares and a chutzpah ensure our longevity and the good-natured attitudes.

What is that incessant shoo-in, an unremitting cliche? Elders revert to their childhood. They speak and act up ASAP. Their engagement in life appears with an offbeat spontaneity, much to the mortification or chagrin of a few folks.

The personal testimonials outshine any displeasure. Confident elders are adamant about the abandonment of something else. The ludicrous idea, the self-sabotage, and any diehard judgments? Arrivederci. Sayonara. "Life is *still* good"—the golden cup of these self-assured elders—is a model for our present world with the unpredictable or unexpected developments.

These upbeat elders grab for the verve, much like our uninhibited children. "Never too late" is their passion to be clinched and repeated, whether or not it is causes the embarrassment or a displeasure with their adult children or any conservative acquaintances.

Courage to express a legitimate concern is another lofty dare. Age does not matter. It is that unfeigned honesty that becomes a definite grabber, gaining the attention and, ultimately, the respect from other human beings.

Our courage to keep-tabs-on—care enough—is an honorable intention. It affirms our nurturance of endearing and valued friends, our siblings, or our parents. All of us are witnesses to today's stories of valuing significant others and cultivating our worldly connections.

Stop judgements, stop complaints, stop something that is unhealthy (we usually fess up), or cease whatever. Simply dare—to forge these uncharted pathways or the healthier rites of passage.

Ready or not? Lifetime lessons appear for all of us. Our readiness, the stamina, a moxie, and an acceptance are re-inventions in certain respects. These untouched, fresh adaptations or virgin approaches hover at our forefront of daily living. When and where do any of us defy the odds and plunge ahead—for a snippet or the smattering of "the unknowns" as our next lifetime lessons?

Our unknown passages are unexplored, remote, or incognito. In essence, each of us explores the "grabber" moments to move beyond our past. There is an urgency to usher in our uncelebrated, unappreciated, and unsung songs.

Our unsung songs? What better time to move forward, given our altering state of affairs in the world?

~~Dare to venture without a walking GPS. Do we really know each statuesque tree, evergreen shrub, beauteous flower, or something else of delight that we missed while zipping along in a car? Forget making an agenda. Temper any of the incessant worries. Release an ounce of the distress that likes to keep company with our worldly scenarios and constant updates.

~~Dare to sketch the self-portraits. Draw 5, 10, and 15 years into the millennium. Sketch intentionally—aiming for a posterity of the striking, upbeat, dazzling, and the confident self-portraits. Giving a fair shake to replenish, refresh, or recreate oneself is a bold dare.

~~Dare to conceive and discover the deserving miracles. Vow to preserve this deep-rooted oath to give birth—to a myriad of serene affirmations. Pause to enjoy these personal re-investments and an inner amnesty.

~~Dare to bring to light and release unconditional love in today's world. No conjectures. Surrender any expectations. Dump the doomsday motives. Let the fearful forecasts fly the coop. Together—we take comfort with our unconditional caring and no regrets.

~~Wake up. Pen a note. "Today, I give myself permission to…" Flaunt a courageous spunk, shift the gears with a prowess, and navigate this day with a fearlessness and another leap of faith. Completion emerges as a highly regarded gift—for our tomorrows.

~~Dare to eat dark chocolate, play unusual music, or nosh on a supreme goodie. Repeat again the next day. Be party to that euphoria, the happy-happy elevation. Give to relief funds, local food banks, and pause to do the random acts of kindness. Let the feel-good endorphins boost your core being and humanity. We soar past an overwhelming angst or the health undulations with these natural lifesavers. These feel-good endorphins are the chemical life-changers. Imagine the ripple effects of our global world being uplifted...

~~Rites of passage are not exclusive to children and adolescents. The nicks, bumps, hurdles, and Herculean efforts at any age are unavoidable. We engage or disengage from the different struggles or strife. We unearth a quality difference by searching for the buoyancy, hopefulness, and a radiant light amidst any layers of darkness.

~~Add a newfangled "grabber" to the daily regimen. Spike up the mundane or humdrum hours. Feel like "full of pep, life, or energy" is not just an exhausted cliche or a triviality. Our worldly encouragement to be creative and seek out the alternatives is transformative.

~~Nothing wrong with grabbing at life's opportunities and the favorable circumstances. Today? Next week? Dare to open our eyes. Dare to catch sight of our nuggets of good fortune. Pass on the good deeds to fellow human beings and witness the positive ripple effects.

~~Dare to delve into a new hobby. Do not pass judgments while navigating any trial-and-error pathways. Seize each minute like it is the last hour on the planet. Pretense creates an ideal space for each of the baby steps during our life's expedition and the unforeseen treks.

~~Snatch a purposeful time allotment each week or month. Dare to discover and chronicle a keepsake or personal memoir. Everyone has a story to archive.

~~The power of our written words is evident. We usually ad lib what happened a few days or months ago. If we left our imprinted words on a page—handwritten or saved as techno-soundbites—there would be our unvarnished truths to witness again. Do we dare?

~~Declare a "grabber" for today. Why not? What is an authentic motivation or an enchantment? Bypass any worries about the random opinions of people at home or in the neighborhood. Even significant folks that claim that they know us might be surprised about our declarative-grabber day.

~~Find a pencil, pen, or colorful crayolas. Dare to doodle or draw on a sketch pad. Vamoose to any artistic constraints. Just let your fingerlings do their natural experimentation. Make time to cherish the Shangri-la...

~~Dare to tackle a real enterprise about your town, a city, or a state. Rise above any challenge. Go online to find out obscure factoids or unusual places that you never knew. Be entertained for a morning or afternoon with your sneak previews as a trailblazing pioneer, a stellar sleuth, or a divine informant.

~~Own a change of heart. Defy any disillusionment or the road blocks that come with our "stay at home" or "close to home" realisms. Tango-on examples greet us on daily television or the Internet. Seek out and explore the yearned-for experiences, particularly before a horde of regrets nestles into your soul.

~~What to do? Who to become? When to show our "new normal" persona? Is today that memorable day or week to seek and find innovative ways to enhance our connections?

~~Remove the window dressing. Remove the veneer. What is left to examine and to improve? Lifelong learning involves taking the gutsy and the valiant actions to shift or flip-flop the ebb and flow of our life's safari.

Life is a
Celebration

HAPPY
THOUGHTS

PEACE
ON EARTH

Happy Birthday

Thinking
of

Let our joys and jubilee strike an impassioned chord…
Acknowledge our desire, the natural human affinity, for the
delightful celebrations—grandiose or small…
No abandonment or the forgotten moments with our evolving world of not knowing…
Uplifting inspirations become a diversion, a treasure, and our solace,
not to be denied—yesterday, today, or tomorrow…

Celebrations and Our Jubilee

A blowout bash. A gala affair. A smashing shindig. Just have a hubbub of a time. Do any of these jubilee affairs strike an upbeat chord?

Dynamite or first-rate recollections often include who attended the euphoric celebration, jam-packed and teeming with the kaleidoscopic images. This exquisite imprinting stays with us for a lifespan. What a bonus to remember—at any time, place, or homestead.

Perhaps, the jokesters come to mind. Every jubilee offers at least a couple of vivacious individuals who are chomping at the bit. Their antics resonate, charm, and beguile all ages at the event. Their humorous one-liners or spellbinding stories are lauded. Without a doubt, the celebration ramps up.

Do we ever slow down enough to be inquisitive or speculate? Why not make the leeway for quality time and these inspirational jubilees during our lifespan? Why procrastinate or wait for a special occasion until the world is back to normal?

The "new normal" means we dignify a decision to make any festive celebration still count. Our remote-internet connections and television still feature these celebrations. Friends driving cars, holding festive signs from the windows, beeping horns, and whatever it takes. The child, adolescent, or adult on the lawn, porch, or at the door is not forgotten, overcome with obvious joy.

On new websites, each of us increases the odds for our positive encounters. We inflate the chances of sublime fortune and a kinship with old or new friends. All of us need to hold fast to that consummate intention—bring on the supreme jubilee in our life's voyage or caravan. Let our manifestations awaken, procreate, and spawn a soul-filled existence. Does it matter that we connect differently in order to protect our human lifespans?

What about the individuals who feel guilty with an extravaganza or a festive togetherness via the earlier or new technology options? What about the folks who do not get off a treadmill—full of angst and perpetual worry?

Number one: each of us owns the 24-karat privilege of choice. Number two: risk-takers dare to taste the golden "spot of tea" throughout their difficult life treks. Number three: adventuresome individuals accept the legitimate ownership of their personal decisions. Number four: The behaviors, new options, and the verdicts of other earthlings are not our responsibility or within a realistic or rightful realm of control. We cannot seize their personal day, the months, or any years for their maverick or a free-thinker spirit.

As I reread this chapter, the PJ free-spirit remains on call. Why? I still cast a vote of "Yes!" Seize a slice of a festive day. My PJ smile, like a Cheshire cat, reappears in a heartbeat.

Did any of us hear the rumor that a smile increases our brain synapses? Just another reason to seize the day.

There is my colorful flashback. The flamboyant signage that I witnessed on the Belt Parkway driving home from Brooklyn, New York lets me smile and chuckle again. Fuhgeddaboudit!

Our world is different now. Which decision is our pegged winner? Do we grab the gusto and celebrate with a jubilance? Or do we—Fuhgeddaboudit?

~~Reflect about the birthday parties of yesteryears. *Birth*day! High time to commemorate the day and beat the drums. High time to glorify the preferential moments and dance to the dynamic musica—envisioned or real.

~~No mandatory requirements for an online ceremony or event? No special reasons? Just be grateful and accept that any peppy and chipper celebration still transforms to the ultra-happy endorphins. These divine peptides let us hang out a wee bit longer on cloud nine.

~~Take ownership of the present. Release the past and our future. Savor and redeem the gift of today. We got your back…let's stay connected…it is our calling… There are televised and talked-about, redeeming messages for all of us during our times of global crises. Absolutely, there is a daily gift for us…

~~Take charge of the dance craving and that fervor. Be feisty and ecstatic. Go ahead! Samba, boogie-woogie, jitterbug, waltz, tap, shimmy, rhumba, jive baby, or do the rock n' roll. If asked why you keep dancing—indoors or outdoors? You *are* the celebration.

~~The science and art of healing meld together. Commemorate this unconventional concoction with a unique participation. Today, I choose to relive…a Native American drumming circle that celebrated the sacred spirit of four. The four directions and winds symbolized a completeness, the universe, and all creation. Today, I make a choice…to magnify and value the symbolism, like the Rock of Gibralter, for our metaphysical awareness, the cultivation, and our like-minded connections. Today or tomorrow? What are your healing choices?

~~Honor, an unconditional love, a trust, the integrity, and those random acts of kindness are exemplary attributes. Take note when a stellar individual with these traits intersects your wayfaring. Pause to experience the undeniable sparks of positive energy and a humanitarian demeanor. Our daily updates, new media-connections, and the "Good Samaritan" stories refresh our memory…

~~Celebrate and honor YOU. No arrogance, simply an acknowledgment of the self-love and a positive regard for yourself, a one-of-a-kind human being.

~~A loving, quintessential anniversary is a cloud-nine jubilee to witness and to embrace. The joyful spirit wants to be present for 365 days. People are still celebrating in very unique ways, often seen virtually—from around the world.

~~Do not give up a blissful memory. I was attending a gleeful parade. People-watching carefully as the procession and fanfare unfolded, I saw an elevated attitude, especially when elated folks were in close proximity. This happy event uplifted the fellow human beings, including myself. Partake, live it up, and be sure to catapult into your mindful-bliss memories. In time, we shall gather again, engage, and create our mindful bliss.

~~The jovial and carnivalesque holidays… The planned or impromptu vacations. The regal or irresistible retreats. All are phenomenal jamborees. The destinations, our dialogues, and raising the bar for amusing indulgences are reserved—as the topnotch champions for our continuous applause. Keep applauding the memories, knowing that festive holiday gatherings are on the be-patient and the safer horizon.

~~ Raise the bar in a nanosecond. Raise the expectation of intriguing diversions. Raise the splendor of gaiety. Raise the unadulterated memory lane. Raise the bar again to recognize and pay tribute to the merriment. Do exactly what the savvy doctors encourage—go for it. Continue to raise the bar, as today's technology opens the once-upon-a-time, unavailable doors.

~~Unpolluted. Unsoiled. Untarnished. Unblemished. Behold and hail the innate treasure of a purified gathering or an indulgent shindig. Each of us owns the fine capacity to recollect and relive. It usually happens when we pay closer attention to a distinct urge or a wish to revisit the celebratory gatherings or our lively shindigs.

~~Radiate a slice of happiness, the kindness, and dote upon the accompanying fulfillment. Share the wealth, which is unsurpassed in dollars and cents. Our mind, body, and spirit cannot wait to reap the loving gifts. Count all of the front-line and behind-the-scenes women and men who give selflessly.

~~Become elated by "something" in this day. Remain hopeful for another day. Be humbled to sustain the elevated feelings. Be honored when an intoxicating pleasure comes full circle—as a lifeline and our keepsake. These values are being professed and affirmed by our world pandemic and our abundance of humane efforts.

~~Celebrate the inestimable seconds. None of us comes with an exact time clock of our lifespan. Tick, tick, tick away—the seconds of our chronological journey. Count down? Count up? A hopeful attitude heralds either way of counting—for our best possible outcomes.

~~No bewilderment, if we seek a triumphant disposition and our undefeated resolve in life. Attitude = altitude.

~~Savor a joyous blast from your past. Recreate an encore of the splendor and those impressive images. Feel the levitation, an uplifting of a far-out, mysterious delight? Be re-awakened with the potential for today's and tomorrow's joy, the charm, and a comforting bliss.

~~Do not outlaw, abandon, or forget. Take a super-colossal suitcase of jubilance and optimism along life's quests, the crises, and those intricate rites of passage. Inevitably, this luggage emerges as our finest tote.

What is more

Health is Wealth

Inner peace arrives as we accept—health is wealth—not a cliche...
What is more—during our daily, conscious living—no longer dismissed...
Affirming ways to lessen worldly plights and enhance our well being...
Seasons of our life—the sublime and real—are not forgotten...

Our Pauses for Renewal

Nope, there is *no juju*. Go ahead and favor a pause or two for the renewal, like a good-luck treasure. Dig into your past recollections that release an instant smile or the head nod. Remember a lucky charm or trinket that became a favorite and your prized souvenir?

Our pauses are also a prized reprieve in a "pandemic world" of semi-chaos and given the non-stop preoccupations throughout our weeks. Yet, our friends and acquaintances share that certain judgements come forth in spite of tougher times, particularly when their intentional pause springs forth.

Certainly not my intention, but… My pauses for renewal are interrupted on different days. I overhear enough conversations on the "speaker-volume" cell phones as I am walking, even with our social distancing. There are the reprimands, nagging remarks, and the raised voices.

Are you doing nothing this afternoon…? Why are you taking that kind of break…? You never could perform well… You need to do much better on school assignments… You did not do well on your last job either… What else did you not finish this week…?

No need to underscore the leftovers from any of these judgement zones. It does not take a rocket scientist. Pauses for renewal and any time-outs are null and void. Not completing whatever task is criticized harshly, never mind the potential completion in one or two days.

Reality-check. What if the pause for renewal is a boost for the family or work-team accomplishments? What if the uncompleted task or tasks is fine to complete on another day or week? If the constant judgments or negative labels pop up, something else happens.

Similar scenarios and these talks happened prior to our world pandemic. The judgements and any inferior labels already gave birth to the personal self-sabotage or a self-fulfilling prophecy. A personal history was in-the-making or pretty solid for a certain child, an adolescent, or even an adult.

No great mystery as to why any of these individuals feel relieved and less guilty or shoddy when they hear that someone else is taking that much-needed break or the pauses. Our former world did not disappear with a global pandemic.

Now? We witness the change-agents of the world. They are credible human beings who offer positive encouragements for the essential pauses, our significant renewals, the health improvements, and our well being. Ultimately, these realistic incentives and amazing boosts serve us well as a better or the best life-balance.

Ahhhhhh! Take quality time to relax and meditate. Take that online class called gentle yoga. Take a power nap to rejuvenate. Undoubtedly, it is a personal choice to halt for an intermission and seek the renewals more frequently.

Is the choice to pause for renewals an old or the new value? It just matters when any of us elect to change—for the self-renewals and to be more capable of giving back to our world.

When any of us agrees to "take a breathing space" on purpose, there is the release of those negative vibes. Like a famous movie nugget—no negative vibes, man. Negativity begets negativity.

Habitual skepticism? No thanks? So, begone—the condemnations, the judgments, the regrets, or the doom-and-gloom attitude. Like today's world, it is beyond "high time" to readjust our pathfinding. Just begin today. Alter our route, seek, and go forward with our esteemed potential for a better life pilgrimage.

Many individuals offer insights on their life-changers, even on the podcasts or new social media. Why? Tune into the experts and that authentic feeling state.

It feels superlative to take ownership of a revival, the stillness, and an inner peace. Our unity and self-love transform into the undeniable renewals. Why not sanctify these sacred feelings of a quietude, a peace, a self-worth, a good will, and our evolving harmony?

~~Decide to make a pit stop from driving to a grocery store, the pharmacy, or a bank. Put on a pair of super comfy, wrap-around sunglasses. Park the car and close those appreciative eyelids. Start to inhale and exhale deeper than any breaths while driving. No hyperventilation, but start to take the deeper breaths. Three times is a culminating charm and tranquility for our rejuvenation. Now, there is more readiness to spread your random acts of kindness that day.

~~Rejuvenation is a superlative 24-karat alternative. It is never too late for the optional time-outs. Cast the die. Call the shots. Decide to own the respect of this first-class choice—for yourself, the family, your friends and significant others, the strangers, and who else? You fill-in the meaningful blanks.

~~I love my human being. I am grateful for the awakening and a re-awakening of my spiritual being. Not evoking and believing these loving-kind words becomes a dismissal and an eviction of self-love.

~~Ego begone. Repeat the mantra. Now, do a gentle touch or a tapping of your heart and the "crown chakra" at the top of your head. Voila! There is a setting free of a healthier spirit and an emotional sustenance for your wellness. At this time period in our "world pandemic" and most of the forecasting news, many of us agree upon less ego and more heart.

~~Debunk the daily stressors. Inhale deeper. Exhale slowly through your mouth with the slightly puckered lips. Try again. Repeat until a "stillness" within your core being comes to light. Patience and practice are mere rhetoric. Try this dynamic duo to debunk the daily or weekly pressures or worries. Patience and practice become our proactive actions.

~~Mindless chatter is simply a human trickster. Drop the 13 inches to your heart. What say thee?

~~Pause. Come to a standstill. Take five minutes. Take ten. Have we forgotten the value and the abundance of this state of being?

~~Enjoy a lull in the action of your "stay at home" or "close to home" scenarios. Take a hiatus, the recess, or a siesta. Do not let any judgments trespass, meddle, or entrench that quintessential space and time. Hey, I see people of all ages taking a snooze in the car, before or after the grocery shopping, any bank business, or the pharmacy pick-ups.

~~Inhale slowly. Feel the tummy puff out? Exhale with a longer breath through the mouth. Feel a stream of air land upon the chest? Repeat. Practice brings forth our "quiet," a serenity, and our peace of mind. Helpful YouTubes and the Zoom meet-ups are also available as our best allies.

~~A comfy, good-feeling chair or couch is ideal. Just unwind or hang loose. Perhaps, there is a settling—into a beloved snooze or the forty winks. Wake up to the epitome of loving-kindness. Pay it forward…

~~Explore the quantum field to actualize the present and the future. An inner, healthy power allows us to shape our quality of life. Given our present state of affairs in the world, how many folks would raise a hand for a lesser quality of life?

~~Slow down. We can slow down as much or as little as we desire. Free spirit remains in the core of our being and our decision-making. Is today the day to put on the breaks? Forego putting our pedal to the metal? In our changing world, controlled and uncontrollable, do we slow down enough? Where is the golden rule book that mandates us to keep up a speed-demon dash or any marathon?

~~Call up the laid-back memories or the permitted locations. Sail, parasail, kayak, or canoe. Forget the completion of a project, incessant worries, or today's must-do lists. Forgetting is not forbidden when a calm on the lake, an ocean, or the river makes its debut. Our presentness and harmony follows suit, perhaps more powerfully on this day or during the next months of our world pandemic and the gradual re-openings. Re-commit to greet and honor this memorable and laid-back quiet. Permit a super recharging of your soul batteries—ad infinitum.

~~Genres of music and lyrics often portray the multi-layers of the "self" and our human experiences. The self who is authentic versus the self who is shaped by our society, the family, and the expectant cliques. The self who is exploring a change and a choice versus the self who stagnates. The self who is mismatched with certain people versus the self that pinpoints the balancing of a free spirit in relationships. Which "selves" prevail in today's spiraling world of change and our blossoming of a unique persona?

~~Create a pose like a "bird of paradise" flower. Move into the fluid movements and culmination of a gentle Tai Chi. Sit comfortably and engage in the meditative breath work. Inhale renewals and exhale the worries to dispel any woes. Attend the virtual classes and practice yoga to enhance an optimal blood pressure. The litmus test? The mind, body, and spirit—all three—appreciate the fearlessness and our committal in times of urgency or a crisis.

~~Hoot and holler at an amazing shooting star. Let go of the kiddo within, permitting the psyche to move from overthinking to that euphoria and the enchantment. Prance, dance, and glorify the awesome seconds of being alive. The universe is not upside-down. Look again... for another shooting star.

~~Deluxe karma defines the quality of our explorations, any breakthroughs, and perhaps, a much-needed revolution or shaking up things a tad. Like each sunrise and sunset, there is a reappearance of the timeless hope for personal budding and our unmistakable sprouting.

~~Zen, our meditation, the meridian flows and our chakras, and other pursuits are touted for today's calm. Virtual classes and varied YouTubes open the windows of opportunity. Professionals bring us to the "teachable moments" and remind us of the Tibetan, Chinese, and Japanese origins. The metaphysical dimensions and our spirit-filled living are existing realms for our re-awakening and replenishment. Be willing to be gifted. Remain open-minded...

**MAKE IT
SIMPLE BUT
SIGNIFICANT**

*Blue Ridge cliffs and mountain range cast the spellbinding wonders…
Entrusting deers in a natural habitat and hawks soar in the
sky-art clouds above my soul-filled being…
Mother Earth Gaia reveals her signs in the quietude of my respectful and earthly presence…
These unencumbered gifts—in the moments of gratuity—touching my appreciative human being…*

Cloud Images and Our Personifications

'Tis a beautiful day. We gaze upward to behold the sky art. The hues from a sunrise or a sunset touch our soul. Our urgency to find the beauty amidst our real and surreal world is legitimate.

In another scenario, we stare much longer at the wispy, cumulous, or extraordinary clouds. The formations speak to us. The appearance or the likeness of a loved one? A replica of an animal face or a body? An iconic imagery?

There are individuals who witness this imagery as a likeness or an awesome photocopy of a person or an animal. Other folks do not see the representation that we point out, even if there is an offering of specific clues. "Look at 1 o'clock. Do you see the profile of a woman with long hair?" We wait patiently, but there is no cloud personification for their eyes to behold.

As our days and weeks pass, there is another sighting. We are swayed in this special moment. Almost literally! The facsimile in the clouds is the spitting image or carbon copy of a significant other in our lifespan.

From that turning point, we are hooked, stopping regularly to marvel at the cloud compositions, any patterns, and the compelling configurations. There are umpteen attempts to scan the skyline, especially for those spitting images of a loved one or even a significant other who is deceased.

There are a multitude of books, related conferences, and ongoing workshops about the "nature signs and cloud images from our loved ones on the other side." Yes, that wording is chosen by the credible professionals. They step up nowadays, coming to us in virtual classes. We learn remotely, but there is our definite desire to tune in.

They are gifted, renowned in their metaphysical fields, and choose to remain in the limelight of today's world. Their selfless acts of giving and offering the free world summits or the affordable classes come to our emails or via the latest social media.

When do any of us start our inaugural event? When do we embark and delve deeper into a relevant online book, a holistic newsletter, or the insightful articles? When do we pay attention to when these informative sessions are provided? Perhaps, when and if our resonance with the cloud images or the nature signs become an integral part of our life questions, a mission, or our aspiring ventures.

Quite frankly, a growing number of individuals are intrinsically motivated. Their attendance and online participation affirm an innate motivation to learn, desire to network, and develop an astute, sensory awareness. No pushes or shoves.

No art of persuasion. No intimidation. Count each of us "checking in" when the inquiries about our attendance are posed. The potential to enhance a further grasp and a mastery of different realms of perception are helpful to juggling and counteracting our newfangled ways of daily living.

My former jet-setting to Toronto, Vancouver, and an Alaskan cruise including five days at Denali National Park held my endless clouds of promise. Window seating afforded the dramatic opportunities to cloud-gaze on a plane, the trains, and our buses. My Mother Nature walkabouts during the cruise and at the famous "Inside Passage" ports permitted a vast skyline for this perpetual imagery.

My inner child wanted the cloud-immersions. I was transported from my window seats into an exotica fairyland. Celestial white, puff-puffery, and curly-cue clouds atop the cavernous cliff sides and near glaciers were awesome. Peeking sunbeams added the breathtaking hues to my cloud facsimiles.

I also witnessed a unique sky art after my eldest sister died unexpectedly. My jet-setting flight was at an altitude of 38,000. An ideal window seat revealed our sister-rainbow, just as I whispered, "Please, don't wait for me, Patti Jo. You already know our love. No more painful hours, just peace for you." But, my beloved sister waited in the intensive care…

Later, I shared my story and questions with a group of experienced pilots and the aviation mechanics. I listened carefully. "It is not possible to see what you did, particularly at that altitude. But—you did. You saw a *rainbow*. How lucky are you! I am going to start watching. Must be your guardian angels…"

Believers… Maybe today's "world pandemic" creates a significant pause to listen to the compelling stories? We often laud and entrust a bona fide storyteller. No halfway beliefs or a dubious, suspicious question. Be assured and credit the credibility of a storyteller—back yonder or right now—with a compelling tale. Most of us are not the wannabes in this firm-believer province.

I shall always believe that my sister was listening to my whispered words with her cloud-bestowal. Shortly thereafter, I spent a day with a friend who was a famous jeweler. I purchased a Mexican fire opal set in a wire wrap. The rough-cut gem was only polished on the front side.

Polishing the backside of the gem meant something else would have disappeared. Wha la! A rainbow, like the rainbow that I witnessed on my high-altitude flight, was obvious on the front side of my wired-wrapped pendant.

Any doubts? Never. I wear this symbolic pendant as my loving Patti Jo remembrance. There is a postscript, the crowning grace for me.

When I arrived home, my sister was still in a coma. Medical experts say the last thing to go is "our hearing." Doctors, nurses, and other allies encourage us to speak to our loved ones and significant others. I believe my story of gratitude was heard, upon my hospital arrival at Patti Jo's bedside.

I have never seen any parallel phenomenon since that day in 2005. My frequent travels included additional flights at that max altitude. The earth-tone hues, the cavern-like images with an exquisite cloud-puffery, and that unforgettable rainbow never reappeared. The "knowns and unknowns" are truly part of our lifelines and our earthly experiences. Each of us elects—to remember or not.

I watch the end-stories on the news channels for the uplifting inspirations. For years, the news anchor's voices and their expressions softened a bit. Today? The loving-kind demeanors, a more gentle cadence in their voices, and the heartfelt messages are congruent with our worldly compassion.

High-level cognitive training for advanced degrees, a capacity to analyze, and that IQ-EQ co-mingle were my former realities. Yet, I did not overthink or obsess about my Patti Jo experience of 2005.

Pure, unadulterated acceptance is not illusive. Neither is our intrinsic motivation. It helped that my EQ—emotive intelligence—allowed me to be perceptive, humbled, and truly grateful. Nowadays? Back to my scanning of the awesome cloud imagery, given our "stay close to home" and the "social-distancing." My Mother Earth Gaia walkabouts are still awesome...

Do we adults still generate the awe of our inner child? Do we still desire the subtle attentiveness of our blossoming adolescence? Do we still yearn for a similar marvel or fascination throughout our adulthood years? Our wonder begets wonder.

~~Watch a movie ahead of reading the reviews. Recall the valued imagery in the movie. During the week, swivel and keep watch. Notice the spectrum of cloud imagery throughout the day into the dusk. Be cognizant of a carbon-copy imagery. Know that a reappearance of a favored illustration, the images, or a likenesses is a rest stop for your soul. Humanity needs these rest stops more than ever...

~~Remember the Seabiscuit movie? I love to view the soulful horse movies again. Standing at a balmy ocean shoreline, here came a golden sunrise. An added bonus was the esteemed imagery. The cloud personification was exactly like Seabiscuit stretching to win—after his miraculous comeback to the racing scene. An unexpected gift? What is showing up in the cloud imagery and your "now" moments?

~~Faces, the full-figures, and an animal image in the clouds become a carte blanche empowerment for our brain. No holds barred. Behold this charismatic appeal, the heartfelt repose, and a hush or calm within our being.

~~Remember and relive. Innovative teachers bring the children outdoors. They offer the encouragements and the discovery learning. Write about those clouds. Textures. Shapes. Animals. People. Write whatever comes to you. Recall the wow-factors? Children acquire an incentive to learn about their free spirit and the amazing creativity. An extra special bonus? The mutual acceptance of a popular cliche and a rallying phrase: think-outside-of-the-box. Let us truly fire up that way of thinking for humankind.

~~Recall the lush, alien world of Avatar... I loved the white-sand footpath to the ocean and my new footprints. Here came a gifting moment—ten o'clock for only 30 seconds—a Terradactile cloud image like the World of Pandora for the Na'vi beings in the Avatar movie. Just a movie? Just a surreal moment and the likeness? The Caribbean-colored, gentle waves continued to touch my bronzed feet, sinking into Mother Earth Gaia. I contemplated that 30-second imagery. Do we still seek the unanticipated moments—in our unanticipated world?

~~We earthlings are observant. Many of us prefer the visual learning for a better association. Our senses escalate in the process. This evolution of the cloud personifications—slowly or quickly appears—for our reception at all ages. A beauty in the clouds gifts us with a gentle nudge. Just like the kids, take a recess—from the past or any futuristic thoughts or misgivings. Do not stray—and miss the cloud artistry and elegance in a mesmerizing, present moment.

~~Ask to see "something or someone" in an ever-changing mural of clouds. Perhaps, a special person whose death was unexpected, too early, or still mourned? Just ask… Accept that a confidence, the patience, and your belief are equal allies with that loving request.

~~Blue skies—an aquamarine, light azure, or the Caribbean hues—often invite a daydream or our deja vu. What do we imagine for an emerging panorama of the clouds on such a stunning canvas? Appreciate our imagination and its serenity.

~~Rainy days. Foggy slumber land. Sunshine caresses our souls in a few days. Sunbeams and the grandiose cloud vistas perk up our spirit naturally.

~~Cloud shapes and the personifications. Our brain engages to analyze, synthesize, and symbolize. Our heart surrenders with the emotive attachments that arise. When our brain is overwhelmed with the world of "breaking-news" and the rising statistics, we need to drop that 13 inches to our heart-anchor for the re-awakenings.

~~Acknowledge the enerCHI—each person's vigor, an efficacy, and a lovely spirit. Golden centuries of Tibetan and Japanese lineages, our connections, and the guardian links to the metaphysical dimensions in today's world are authentic. Our kindred and human spirit is capable of manifesting a positive regard for these renowned and quintessential re-awakenings.

~~The earthly dimension of Mother Earth Gaia offers a grounding. Let your feet feel her welcome. Our crown or head chakra represents a pure consciousness. Our humanness, inclusive of this grounding and a higher spirit, permits us to be the transformative risk-takers and the compassionate guardians of humanity.

~~Be a sky-scanner. Be a cloud-catcher. Behold the communiques, sustained or even fleeting. These Zen-like and etheric signs permit an uncommon quality of knowing—for our highest good.

~~EnJOY a lakeside memory… A smile-crescent moon is high in the angelic-like clouds. Dreamscape and awaken. From a tent closer to the shoreline, you watch intently. Nature bequeaths the prism-waves and the fly-by birds. Welcome, your salmon-golden sunrise. A rainbow reflection caresses another wave, only for a few seconds and your aurora-morning gift.

~~Respect our eagle-eyes. Rounded puffery and brilliant-white, cumulus clouds greet us. The stratus and gray-like clouds appear like the fog on a horizon. The wispy-curly-hair cirrus clouds arrive. This cast of characters is a nature-veil across the skyline. Faces and imagery in this stunning celestial-sphere promise to elevate and make our day. All of us still desire and need that life-balance.

~~An attitude of gratitude happens with a mere glance upward. Changing hues and our sky art form on a multitude of days. The sun-dog clouds present us with fragments of the rainbow colors. When sunlight passes through the ice crystals, refracting horizontally, any of us can pause to be enchanted with its spectral colors. Left or right of our sun. Here comes the grandeur of the cloud imagery and the rainbow manifestations. Live and enjoy...

~~Contemplate the faces witnessed in the clouds. Known or unknown? Cherub, guardian, or the archangels? Divine images or the infinite souls? Are we believers of providence and these premier angels? Will the angelic messengers guide, imbue, and love us unconditionally, whenever we meet for our inaugural and pioneer moments?

Vintage lights press against the different stucco textures…
The striking-blue florals still manage to bow and curtsy nearby…
Invitation granted—to see the unexpected beauty emerging…
Like a new inheritance—the perfect imperfections—now in
accord with an acceptance and our daily living…

Our Perfect Imperfections

P erfect. The word conjures up something else. Heebie-jeebies, the bizarre expectancies, the past or present anxiety, or kicking up a notch or two of feeling totally inadequate or incomplete.

"Are you kidding? There is no such thing as perfect." "Where have you been living—in La La Land?" "That word gives me pangs of stress, never mind trying to become perfect or superior." "Oh ya, my brother (sister) is always perfect (infallible) in my parents' eyes." Across the decades of teaching, I was entrusted with not only the soundbites, but also the personal stories about perfection.

I digress momentarily. During the initial months of our world pandemic, we were the human beings who yearned for a more perfect world. "Yearning for a more perfect world" was our wanton phrase for valid reasons. We were blindsided and feeling shocked, horrified, and somehow estranged, way beyond "yesterday's world" of perfect imperfections and those candid memories.

Yet, the perfect imperfections and yesterday's complaints or any rebuttals were important, especially when I was first composing this book. A year later? The daily soundbites, our escalating statistics, and the next forecasts of a spiraling "second-wave" garnered our utmost attention.

Pause for a minute… Perhaps, the titanic waves of vulnerability, the panic-stricken feelings, and a real distress underscored our perfect imperfections? The "new normal" did not change the inferiority feelings in our past history. Each of us still owned the familial, the educational, or the societal labels and the earlier messages and our pigeon holes.

During my career in the university settings, I never ran out of my students' remarks or opinions about the hindrances or the virtues of perfection. Traditional or non-traditional ages did not matter. Their gender or cultural beliefs made their tote—an incredible baggage of desired perfections—an ingrained, recurrent, or the accepted reality.

Perfection was indeed a sought-after utopia. Yet, perfection launched the number of times each individual's stress-meter would definitely sky-rocket. Was it the year or the season to switch gears? Was it a decisive month or a specific week for a personal metamorphosis?

Who wants the sky-rocketing distress associated with the obvious signs and symptoms that adore the company of supreme perfection? Where and when does the perfecto-syndrome land "ever so perfectly" in any of our life prospects, our presumptions, or our preferred journeys?

A myriad of unanswered questions surround any individual's perfection cycle. Unless, a person chooses to slow down. Then vote for a showdown—reject the dire forecasts, any tiresome commotions, and the monotonous melodramas that come with any perfection ultimatums.

Few of us are in love with the word "imperfection." Yet, many of us are darn good and ready to admit that all humans are capable of mistakes. Besides, at least a million or billion folks are quick to nod in agreement. It is quite simple. All of us cannot be off-base, right?

Drudgery? Rat race? Finally—defy the doldrums, the blues, a malaise, or horrific dejections that accompany any perfection. Calling one's bluff begins to feel much better. Perfect imperfections sounds kosher, believable, and sane.

Our adoption of "perfect imperfections" makes common sense. Plus, it feels healthier to release any unsettling and intrusive regrets. Once and for all, we are playing with a full deck. No matter what is happening in today's world with serious burdens and entanglements, we often own and still confront our leftovers. Leftovers? Our totes or personal baggage—that love to come along for any ride.

Enough! Several of us take another leap of faith. We proceed with an acceptance that each of us owns a medley of human imperfections. Now is the time to shift the gears, transition, and change. This reality is way beyond a shadow of a doubt. Do we truly need a reminder in our unpredictable world, chock full of the "we do not know..." comments or the testimonials?

Let go of an absurdity and the energy-zaps that accompany any race or that marathon to attain perfection. Several individuals hazard a guess or brainstorm. Enough of us start to muse, surmise, or contemplate. We wonder why the realizations and pure relief took so long? No worries. Our arrival at the opening doors to self-improvement is what matters.

Self-improvements happen throughout our lifetime. Hopefully, we are the wiser souls in this life-cycle quest with our abandonment of perfection. If there is a group of like-minded folks that we seem to have missed earlier, there is a maturing acceptance that we are willing to stretch. New beginnings...

New beginnings warrant a collective mindfulness in our present world. A green light. Admission. Consent. An acceptance of "going forward together" manifests a more authentic way of living, far beyond the mere lip-service.

As I pause to reread and put forth those intentions, one of my epiphanies comes full circle. "An eagle soars above the odds. Why not you?" It is not the time for any of us to detour from this moving-forward momentum—as individuals and as change-agents committed to our world.

~~None of us is perfect. Expectations of supremacy and faultlessness heighten our anxiety and the steady cycles of self-sabotage. The legendary and influential cliche—to err is human—creates a prosperous space for self-love.

~~Seven decades are on the horizon. As I am writing this epiphany at 67 years young and moving forward, I am wiser. There is an acknowledgment and a genuine affinity of PJ's perfect imperfections. I celebrate Sat Nam, the radiant light of "I am" throughout a lifespan. May our global connections remain full of human beings who honor this radiant light, continuing the humanitarian efforts and the positive renewals.

~~Say the word—forgiveness. Each of us owns the flaws and shortcomings. We need to pay forward our capacity to seek and find the new beginnings. Kindred souls in need are able to reap the benefits from our amplified process of overcoming and sharing our pathfinding.

~~My parents lived to 96 and 97, just shy of their 74ᵗʰ Anniversary. Depression, World War II, the loss of a first-born infant, and financial-health burdens arrived within the span of a decade. An unexpected death of the eldest daughter, the 13-year albatross and sorrow of Alzheimer's, and other Herculean trials became their real-world experiences. Across these decades, it was unconditional love, trust amidst the chaos or traumas, and a dogged determination that became their legacy.

~~ Forgiveness. Easy to give our lip service. Ditching or ejecting the leftover expectancies of perfection creates a leeway for something special—our capacity and ownership to forgive others.

~~Unveil the layers of self-doubt about any of the perfect imperfections. Use a different compass. Decide to forsake the schleppin' around or the backtracking attitude. Secure the steadfast strides and hike forward. Pick up the pace for today's world. Build a bridge of faith across each gorge, a chasm, or the crevasse.

~~ Deep abyss or the black holes? Toss colossal hope and inspirational values to the wind. Entrust that the void or our gaps will be filled to the brim again…

~~His fancy, imagination, and free spirit. Her vision, pipe dreams, and independence. Siblings and friends are not always on the same wave length. Perfect imperfections? Change our bird's eye view and our prospects. Try again for the humane connections.

~~Unexpected hurricanes, wild fires, mud slides, or the earthquakes. No promises of a perfect world. Yet, these sweeping and protracted traumas tend to re-connect human beings. Our random acts of kindness in a town, city, state, or the world often appear spontaneously.

~~Our Richter scale of emotions heightens. Perfection. Is there more or less escalation? Deliberate pauses for a reality-check? Is it easier and more comfy to let whichever action—escalation or deliberate pauses—take over? There are no mandates for a heartfelt re-direction. A personal choice awaits…

~~We learn that perfection is an unspoken or subtle norm, a destiny to pursue. Suspicions ring true. Signs are overt. "Oh, _____, you can do *much better* than that!" Fill in our namesake. Then confess to the guilt-trippin' mania—unless a new effort to stop and change gets our head nods. Our perfect imperfections become palliative, a soothing balm. Our serenity is more likely to be shared.

~~Human beings often express their concern about the below-par perfections. Time for reconsideration? Then put forth the efforts to greet more contentment. Practice self-forgiveness. That action becomes the best truth serum and welcome immunization.

~~Seize a day for the new beginnings. Try a lighten-up mantra with a meditation. This effort becomes an act of trust. Confidence and conviction transform into our positiveness and a hopeful attitude. Are we not searching for the unmistakable, confident, and affirmative vibes in our ever-changing world?

~~Instant gratification? Well, we are supposedly the grown-ups, not the adolescent or a child. However, it is a prime time in our global watch to re-examine our life station. Do we overhear that someone else at our age actually feels lucky? How did we miss our charmed moments? It is not too late for better options and the alternative ways of living.

~~My telepathic messages arrive. Where-to-look comes simultaneously. Almost surreal, given that it happens without the delays. Divine or omniscient guidance for every earthling, even with our perfect imperfections? Our human capacity with the metaphysical dimensions of the divine, angelic, and spirit-filled guidance is touted. The YouTubes and credible websites are available for this mindfulness. A personal choice—to become mindful or enlightened?

~~Contentment. A softer repose. We like who we are, accepting the noticeable blemishes or our eccentricities. No insincerity, hype, or make-believe. No sham or subterfuge. We do not fake our contentment and this comfort. We choose to reject any presumptions of the utopia or a paradise of perfections.

~~Flawless. Unmarred. Unsullied. Foolproof. Finally, we are comfortable, untroubled, healthy, and pleased—in our own skin.

~~Be perfect or be something else. The option of a free-spirit mentality and the matching actions prevail in our fast-lane world of the trials and tribulations. Notice the rave reviews about a free spirit. Applaud the alternatives on today's podcasts and diverse websites. Elect to change? Clap heartily, with a standing ovation, for our newest ownership of bravado and complementary actions.

A gift of animal pals is inspirational with our companionate and our untethered connections…
Our first-to-last bonds resonate wholeheartedly, remain steadfast in our mind, body, and spirit…
There is rarely a facade, resistance, or the dis-connections…

Animal Pals and Our Bonding

Think of our animal pals. Here comes a smile and the warm fuzzies. Our connections begin pronto. Unconditional love, amazing trust, our playtime, and the indelible phenomena of our animal-human communication do not wind down.

Take notice of the phenomenal increase with today's individuals and family who are rescuing or purchasing the animal companions. Rescued dogs appear on television moments—the precious expressions with our adoptions.

These amazing and front-line employees are working, not remotely but at many on-site facilities, so that the record number keeps escalating. More stories show the immediate bonds that elicit the "wow and astounding" comments.

Undoubtedly, these devout rapports are morphing into "till the cows come home" and priceless memories of new companions during our traumatic and challenging times. Other animal lovers are recapturing a vivid memory lane. We cannot own dogs where I live, but my neighbors in the condo complex still relish and recount their glorious and fun-filled memories. I was no exception.

Patches became my first dog, a wire-haired terrier with an attitude that I was smitten with—for years. Actually, she was picked out by the entire family. My mother had severe bouts of asthma with horses, dogs, and cats. Our homestead needed a super dog, but a breed that did not shed.

Suckers from the get-go. All of us chose Patches and left with a menagerie of doggy stuff in this tempting store. Patches radiated an electrifying, mesmerizing demeanor. Shortly thereafter, I had another magnificent opportunity.

Stable chores, riding lessons, and other kiddos who wanted the lucky chance and a fair shake. Finally, I rode the American Saddlebred mare, a chestnut beauty that pranced and high-stepped naturally. Vickie Gale became a similar touchstone, my next animal pal and forever love.

Yah, my parents supported me at the horse shows. Mom would have to sit in the air-conditioned car, but cheered as loudly as the rest of the family. I never inherited her asthma. Much later in life, when I lived in Texas, my decision was a piece of cake. I was like today's kindred spirits who are adopting or buying their animal pals in spite of any world scenarios. My best-ever memories are not lost.

My first dog was gonna be a colossal one. Entre' Beaugart, a 75-pound Shepard. Traditional black and tan colors. That was where the tradition ended. He was bored with more than 10 minutes of training.

Potty-trained ASAP. Beau was a smarty, plus the ultimate diehard for any kind of games. He came everywhere in my Chevy pickup until...

Entre' his buddies—Butchie-e-e, the eventual 19-pound, lovely Tom cat and Rocky, a 125-pound Shepard of sable distinction. His golden-luster heart glowed for miles.

These three musketeers gave the maudlin looks—we must ride and travel *everywhere* in your pickup, Mommy. Our loving bonds brought tears of joy and exuberant laughter. Pardon me for pausing, but do any readers identify with this scenario—biggie time, perhaps?

I am still catching sight of the blissful dogs riding in cars to the grocery stores, the banks, or pharmacies. Have yet to see the doggie-masks though? It is obvious that these animal pals—young or aging—are making a daily difference in the quality of unconditional love and offering a precious life-balance during our global pandemic. I continued to relive my stories when I witnessed their joys.

Were the three musketeers in the Texas homesteads the end of my animal pals? Hardly. Like a lot of folks, when an endearing animal-pal passed onto heavenly bliss, there was a fine critter that arrived on the cue.

My rescue of newborn Bullwinkle was on the dirt roads in north central Texas. He was dumped and would not live. He was a mix of Shepard and coyote.

Mama Rocky and Butchie-e-e rose to the occasion. No give-away of this pint-size dude. Everyone declared, "You need another dog. Think of the hysterical baths. Plus the collar and toys that you already bought him. Oh, look at his soft brown eyes!"

Then came the next advocacy, the unified voices of my infatuated friends and enraptured neighbors. "Stop trying to find a home for Bullwinkle!" Of course, the fated bonding happened. My nuts-about-you-guys stories and our unconditional love never left my glowing heart.

Today's renewals? There are touching movies, YouTubes, compelling books, and the spellbinding photography—available online or via our television. They capture the bonds, worth a King's or Queen's ransom, between animal pals and human beings. Some folks own additional memories of animal pals and their value. Again, I was no exception.

I also cherished the irreplaceable and vivid recollections of engaging dogs that came to my Dad's facility. The label of "severe Alzheimer's" never detracted from the bonding that I witnessed with my Dad and his new companions. Both men and women in his "severe and locked unit" calmed down with these loving, therapeutic dogs or the music venues presented by talented volunteers.

I remain a devotee, a firm believer. Childhood, adolescence, and adulthood are no exceptions. Research and watching these lifetime interactions validates this bestowal of the animal pals and our human connections.

An inconceivable harmony, the interrelationships, and a similar wavelength are authentic. Is our world resurgence and picking out the "special" animal pals teaching us more than we ever envisioned? Our bonds are dynamic and indicative of a heartrending simpatico...

~~We bond. Our animals become the earth angels. Their unconditional love stays in the "now."

~~No doubts. Little need for approval or agreement. Just watch with an open mind and heart. Animal pals exude that all-knowing spirit of each and every one of our emotional vibrations.

~~A new-found friend expressed his love for Ally. She lived a long life for a dove. For almost two decades, this pet dove became his "godsend and entrusted pal." What a boost and inspiration for today's world of angst! There is a re-awakening with our "godsend" or beloved animal pals.

~~Animal buddies are an irrefutable life force. No price tags. Just count all the soul-filled years, the dedication, and our abundant fortune.

~~Ever watch the European Lipizzan horses? Find a virtual tour, a YouTube, or the online book. Magnificent dressage performances. Feats beyond belief. The appreciative equestrians and Lipizzan partners take years and quality time for schooling, this alliance, and an interdependent bonding. That essence of "togetherness" is an exemplary model for our worldly connections.

~~Squirrels loved the front lawn near our dormitory. They scampered and dashed 'round and 'round the bigger rock-seats. The "nut-tossing" playtime and our bonds came during all seasons of our collegiate years. Meet-ups at the rock-seats were a tad chilly in the New Hampshire winters. Bravado playtime was worth every second. Who became your animal playmates—yesterday or in the "now?"

~~Bird feeders promise to bring our companions. Try a stemmed flower in your mouth. Patience. Behold the quivering hummingbirds that risk the extraordinary, near-sighted visits. More patience. Our gift of hummingbirds is coming again.

~~A lively woman lived alone. She purchased one kitten and rescued two kittens. Each of them sensed her disability, never left her alone. They became her godsend and an opportunity for her reciprocal caregiving. Reciprocal caregiving dignifies our lifetime lessons.

~~Precious bonds are rare. Our animals are the devoted mentors that teach us. These animal pals reaffirm the innate values of tolerance, an unequivocal love, and a complete trust.

~~Neighborhood animals are not always immediate friends. An intriguing lifetime lesson? They learn the art of tolerance, resilience, and the potential for bonding better than most human beings.

~~Our pals from the animal kingdom sense our emotions like depression, sorrow, and intrinsic joys. No psychiatrist, psychologist, Marquis award, or a bombardment of advertisements are needed for this validation. We are witnesses of this validation of similar emotions with today's soul-filled world.

~~Witness the service dogs that are approved to visit an Alzheimer's facility or the nursing homes. Different breeds bring a calm, even to the most severe, locked units. As a devoted caregiver, I watched my beloved Dad in the dementia and severe Alzheimer's units. Almost immediately, the owners' walkabouts and greetings with their earth-angel dogs became an offering of amazing grace. Life changed. Our pandemic invaded these facilities with a vengeance. Let us send forth an amazing grace to those elders in today's nursing homes and their significant others.

~~Genuine animal-human connections bring forth the walloping smiles and our storytelling. Treats and water dishes set near shops, boutiques, and outdoor cafes attest to the doggie "welcome mat." Peek at the Lilliputian infants in carriages or inside the tote bags. Surprise—a Cheshire cat or Snoopy dog steals our heart. We engage effortlessly. Never forget to let these superlative moments sneak into our days and weeks.

~~A dragonfly signifies a good omen. This morning, a golden dragonfly appeared. It hovered and flew low, closer to my hand gesture and gentle voice of invitation. Late afternoon, after a hassle with a rental-scenario and zooming cars on the interstate, a radiant glow greeted me—two golden dragonflies. My uplifted spirit and hand gesture happened in a New York minute. Do we pause, respect an inspirational moment, and remember that soothing blend of our mindfulness and a captivated spirit?

~~Looking up, a mere 15 seconds. First, the commanding cloud personifications. Second, a dazzling, orange-gold sunset. It shines perfectly above a drifting sailboat on a serene river. Do we recall purposefully—these split-seconds of masterful artistry? "Social distancing" is not stopping my appreciation of cloud imagery and the sunsets during my walkabouts with colorful masks. "Back at home" means the split-second moments or minutes to pull my chair near my patio door or my front window to see this beauty transforming…

~~Today, I was off a bubble. Too much world pandemic, so I paused. Ah, of course—my "animal pal" memory for a mini-reprieve. Yes, a superstar. First came the "amazing feats." A small ball, tossed out to the ocean with pounding waves, beckoned an Olympian event for this Labrador Retriever. For at least an hour—impressive recoveries of the disappearing, tidal-wave ball. This stealthy black lab was a 10-PLUS. Unfathomed with the rip-tide propulsions. Energy to the max. Only we mortals—the fan club—became breathless. Meanwhile, the Olympian Labrador was already seeking out another strong-armed fan. Who me? C'mon, will ya be my next playmate? Well, I am an animal whisperer, so I heard that request and grabbed the best playtime. I am still belly-laughing. Just now, a dude was walking by my parked car with pint-sized dog. Those doggie-legs were movin' and groovin' at wharp-speed to keep up. A "today" moment that I could have missed, but did not. Yay!

~~Make it a daily habit—see the scenario as a replaying video. Maybe it is a phone video to rewatch? Early morning and a beach stroll. Bait fish galore and the esprit de corps of two pelicans, enjoying a gulch-camaraderie. Imagine these focused pelicans in the *shallowest* of ocean waters. Never witnessed, up close, and rather hypnotizing for me. This pelican-human connection prompted something else. My dearest, childhood buddy gifted me a rock with Carpe Diem—seize the day—painted on the top. On a shelf that united my condo kitchen and cozy cafe, it became my loving-kind touchstone. Seize each *and* every day, PJ...

~~Upgrade. Break through. Step-up the momentum. Spend quality time with our animal friends, the loyal companions through the humps, bumps, and any zingers in our life treks in this ever-evolving world. Just a dog, horse, cat, bird, or another animal pal? Never...

GO
live
YOUR
life

Be yourself

Our tango-on spirit simplifies living and our intentions…
Be yourself, owning that exquisite comfort and a sense of worth…
Let the Grand Tetons and crystals resonate with beautific reminders…
Reach higher to fill your cup, full to overflowing with the worldly and unconditional connections…

Tango On and Our Altitude

In 2014, I composed a book entitled, "Tango On: Attitude = Altitude." My rereading stimulated the eureka moments, permitting today's altitude to strengthen my thoughts and actions. Then and now, the universal appeals resonated. I was not alone, not in our present-day world of the pandemic and news broadcasts.

Everyone owns a story. Actually, our inheritance of the stories multiplies across a lifespan. We retain the title and become the full heir to a potpourri of memories. So how does each of us fair?

How does each of us cope and "tango on," knowing that today's peaks and valleys befriend us on any day, week, or the months ahead? There are suspected "second waves" in the early fall or winter months, televised protest rallies, and the gradual or abrupt changes in state mandates. The too-soon warnings of our virus spikes and the breaking-news imagery are a foreshadowing.

Together, we strive and continue to coach one another. Yet, everyone needs to draw upon a former "tango on" spirit in their life experiences, a determined pathway, and the positive outcomes.

Decades ago, I shared the PJ "tango on" spirit with my parents, sisters, and significant others. They were anxious, worried, and overwhelmed for good reasons. The health challenges, my survivals, and the new lifestyle accommodations were my looming realities.

How would PJ alter this rugged trek with the daily ravines, especially since my journey was spanking new? Guts. Perseverance. Trial and error. Journaling. Renowned hospitals and lauded centers for healing. Finding the docs—who sweat it out or quit cold turkey.

Yes, there were my excessive searches and countless quests to defy the grim predictions. The next horizons? More empathic and determined health professionals. Healing energies. Holistic alternatives. Meditation and mantras.

Daily and yearly strife, new challenges, and the trials continued. *Give it your best shot. Do not lose sight of the dogged, hang-tough attitude, PJ.* I plugged away to remain open-minded, amidst all of the imposing steps backward and forward.

Find the damn peaks, PJ. Search high and low, leave no stone unturned…

For any of us who share these dicey health-journeys, there is at least one truth. The gestalt or "wow" seconds bobbed up or barged right into our rocky, unsettling journey. No fairy or leprechaun was there to wave a magic wand or grant a wish. No loving human beings—family, siblings, or significant others—were able to dismiss, reverse, or overrule the rugged terrains that we encountered.

Gridlock? Impasse? Be brave and confront? Brace for certain remnants sticking around? Defy any of the odds? It was my individual choice—to "tango on" for many years. *Rise above, PJ. Tango on. Beat the odds...*

I looked to my treasure trove. Positive years were not taken for granted in my family. When the wayfaring trials arrived on their horizon, my decisive parents fell head-over-heels in love again. My observant and empathic Madre and JJ adopted and valued a PJ "tango on" spirit and encouraging outcomes.

Beating the odds, a positive mindset, the au courant passion, and the up-to-the-minute moxie served them mightily. There were earlier and serious "tango on" scenarios—back surgeries, asthmatic undulations, and a challenging tumor. That PJ "tango on" spirit? It was talked about and heightened during their last decades of togetherness. There were additional "unknowns" like Alzheimer's that sprang forth. In spite of the utmost challenges, my endearing and feisty Madre and JJ lived to 97 and 96 years young.

Separation during World War II, unexpected deaths of a stillborn infant and eldest daughter at 62, financial undulations, and health challenges became other compelling tests of fortitude and resolution. Just imagine—how a seasoned spirit of "tango on" consoled and served their partnership during those daunting experiences—just shy of their century mark. Parental battles, PJ battles, your own private or shared battles, and now, a world-rival pandemic to battle?

Our "now" means another kind of relentless battle, equally as daunting with the spiraling and flattening-curve history. Inevitably, our seasoned spirit joins us from any memoir of our imposing and challenging life safari.

Our need for "togetherness" comes full circle. Each day, every week, and the ongoing months reaffirm our collective expertise and the "tango on" efforts. Our best passages and the hopeful boulevards are revealed. Better avenues that are being figured out for the ultimate safeguarding, our preservation, and humanity are witnessed. They become visions of the forthcoming legacy of hope and optimism.

~~Ego begone. Repeat the mantra on a daily basis. Applaud this awareness of contingency plans for the healthier life quests. Be a wanderlust navigator or a globe-trotter in unorthodox ways—take those virtual travels, explore the next vacation plans on the Internet, and keep a visionary journal log. Our verve, willpower, and boldness do not evaporate with our adaptations. Meanwhile, a personal "tango on" spirit and our "togetherness" serve us well.

~~Any day or week is a self-challenge, but not impossible. Abandon the darkness. Take baby steps without the baggage of self-judgements. Seek counsel and the like-minded friends or family for comfort, peace, and the higher-quality options. Like-minded allies befriend one another to elevate, welcome, and triumph the combined genius. All of us dignify the humanitarian efforts and astounding signs of an optimism, the hopes, and a resilience for our better quality of life.

~~Manifest your comfort zone with a daily attitude of gratitude. Look around in our versatile, refashioning, and recalibrating world. There are always supportive survivors and esteemed role models to behold, respect, and emulate.

~~Slow up a frenzied pace, the Catch-22, or any stalemate. Quality time and our enterprising spirit matter. Travel onward or push forward with a resourceful or offbeat passion. Cultivate the networking and connections with valuable allies.

~~Vamoose. Scat. Skiddoo. Hightail it, ego mania. Make a forceful commitment to release the overthinking about the chaotic or bygone years. At that time, the litmus test of "tango on" befriends us, particularly on behalf of our cognitive and emotional well being. Our witnessing of the "tango on" spirit still prevails in today's worldly summons.

~~Stretch with the innate, heartfelt feelings. Stretch beyond the ultimate spandex. Our sense of humor and not relinquishing its value tenures a melding of harmony and a re-awakening, motivating a spirit for daily living.

~~The tango is an ambitious dance to master. "Tango on" is an expression, a mindset, and a demeanor. It manifests as the ultimate gift of loving-kindness towards oneself.

~~Volunteer. Support relief efforts. Helping one, two, or a host of human beings multiplies the dividends beyond our wildest fantasy. Magnifico!

~~Stretch your body at the virtual gym. Exercise at home or during a daily walkabout or power walk. Stretch your mind with an ultimatum or a dare. Stretch your intuition, a valuable commodity with the winning namesake—our sixth sense. Keep on stretching—for the anticipation, the confidence, the prospects, and an optimism about our future.

~~Take more than 30 seconds for a character check. Yesterday? Today and tomorrow? Seek to maintain the "natural high" mindset. Make elbowroom and leeway for a purposeful, positive mood and revealing a vibrant aura throughout each day. Our natural-high vibe and our aura are truly witnessed by other individuals.

~~Bargaining chips, power plays, imposing attitudes, and the controlling agendas do not create the warm-fuzzies climate in our work settings. Ring a bell? On-site or working remotely? Flash back to the unmistakable nonverbal clues. Not exactly a group of happy campers? Our colleagues affirm what they craved—to ditch or desert that work environment. Time to "tango onward" or dance to a new drummer? New vibrations? Different boulevards with a "fine tuning" of our career-footprints are a choice. Remember…when the opportunity presents itself again.

~~The tango is a spellbinding dance to behold. Our feisty spirit of "tango on" manifests an unparalleled beauty and a charm. Remote and internet connections still offer opportune moments for a similar gift-giving.

~~Do any of us really have a hankering for a crystal ball? A mystical ball lets us off the hook of wondering about the yin and yang in our life. Imagine saying, "Begone"—to any disturbing or trying syndrome. No worries, mate. Maybe in our next lifetime?

~~Positive outlooks are contagious. Feel the psychological and physiological uplifting in the presence of people who exude these infectious vibrations? Feel an emotional sinking in the presence of people who emit the negative vibes about almost everything in life?

~~Attitude makes a difference. Generations acknowledge this universal philosophy and valid appeal. FaceTime? Recollect your interactions with the young elders whose age is deceptive. Next FaceTime? Listen to brilliant parts of their oral history, chock full of winsome attitudes, regardless of what life forces came to pay them a visit or two.

~~Memory is a wondrous gift. Remember catching the bennies? Sea mist waves or lapping-lakeshore waves? We are still allowed in a nearby lakeside park. Neon signage reminds us of "social distancing" and "being safe." My intermittent and nostalgic visits add to my memory bank. An amazing grace of healing, purposefully touching my soul again...

~~Our urgency? Excessive everything? We are capable of being the take-charge earthlings—chasing 'round and bird-doggin' everything. One day blends into the next week, month, or year. But, a "tango on" momentum encompasses something else beside a frenzied-everything syndrome. A tireless determination in the company of the quality-breathing time. This tango-on energy uplifts, never undermines or zaps our best intentions and patience. My 24-carat commitment? Continue to own this spirit-filled energy, best intentions, and patience for our global world.

~~Bring along our chutzpah at every chance. Hit the jackpot. Snatch a cavalier fearlessness—a frisky, bubbly, and spunky willpower—for each venture, endeavor, and our enterprise in daily living.

Disquieting times of war and horrific images did not infringe
upon a profound and an unconditional love…
A communal spirit of partnership—for them and their daughters—
was never forgotten, nor taken for granted…
Freedom to sing along, dance any which way, and set loose a free
spirit was spotted, admired, and encouraged…
Significant others who visited frequently became the inclusive companions of
a horizon—their love, a whimsy, the talks, and the giving spirits…

Living Our Soul-Filled Journey

Are we impassioned, expressive, or ardent? Are we genuinely living the soul-filled journey? Inevitably, there are refreshing flashbacks that crop up. A celebrated and impressive age? Maybe, an unforgettable saga in our lifespan that engenders a smile or our storytelling. The big-league "warm fuzzies" reappear.

Did we label any of these milestones as soul-filled? Did this lingo, living the soul-filled journey, even exist? Perhaps, we were knowledgeable or just unaware. Undoubtedly, we are "plugged in" with the "stay at home" and "stay connected" messages that appear repeatedly on the daily newscasts.

Ensure a life-balance during the daily crises, especially with the these simulcasts about our exponential statistics. Pursue a relaxing venue or a virtual tour, enjoy the heartfelt podcasts, or read an appealing genre of your choice. Go online to read or search your dusty bookcase, cubbies, or shelves to unearth the gem for a weekly reading.

How many years ago, not just today? There are a plethora of books and the e-books. Recently closed bookstores designated the self-help aisles for the nonfiction, the fiction, New Age, Zen, the metaphysical dimensions, the angelic realms, and our well being. Pertinent titles were placed purposefully.

Throughout this world pandemic, our libraries are closed for the public safeguards, but the technology still beckons us, if reading interests are a welcome diversion. Kindle readers, the mini-readers with your favored genres, or our purchase of new or the used books on various websites are definitely the healthy reprieves and tempting diversions.

I was able to go into a neighborhood bookstore, until mid-March. Certain things remained unaltered. The front covers of books faced patrons, almost as if they could jump off the top shelves. The touted, contemporary phrases used on these prominent book titles faced outward rather than vertical to catch the ultimate attention of the patrons.

Gurus and guruettes were (still are!) the acclaimed authors. It was definitely a no-brainer. Each of us indulged to nourish and treat ourselves. There were other earth-angels standing near us or sitting in the cafe sipping coffee or organic teas that were equally intrigued. Perhaps, they began to engage with us in a thought-provoking conversation, seeking our common lingo and taking a shine to the relevant information.

No puzzlement, daze, or a bewilderment, particularly when we visit those bookstores again. Tomorrow holds promise—the hope and an optimism to revisit a favorite haunt. Why? I speak for myself and the other kindred spirits. We shall return and feel the "warm fuzzies" again, when the green light beckons us.

Imagine and recapture that essence of yesterday. Do not stop envisioning our future. Imagination and anticipation are still alive… We are urged to find "our tribe" in a contemporary jargon. These like-minded earthlings want to share—the relevant and alluring readings, meaningful workshops, splendid retreats, and the training venues. They covet that essential and former desire to affirm our human quest—to seek, master, flourish, and evolve. Live that soul-filled life…

Voila! Just a bookstore? Just random folks in those designated aisles or yearning to dialogue in the cafe or near the book shelves? No overthinking and any outwitting attempts are imperative or even necessary.

Another no brainer, especially whenever *and* wherever a cosmic epiphany springs forth—the "now" becomes a looking-forward time for our re-openings. That defining moment of our "new beginnings" also re-awakens, inspiring and comforting us that we are not alone.

~~Lingering coffee breaks and the dinners with a significant other are a treasure trove. Squeeze in the opportunity for a soul-filled reprieve that elevates each other unequivocally. None of the ifs, ands, or buts. Each of these lovely and "spot on" rendezvous catapults into our clairvoyant memories.

~~Lessen the whining and that woe-is-me syndrome. Take charge. Replace any of the grumbles, daily complaints, weekly gripes, or even the snivels with a tenacity. Fearlessness, a boldness, our backbone, and an audacity are all part of an esteemed chutzpah or a bravado. Take note of our worldly chutzpah. Our "togetherness" messages are the imprints forevermore…

~~Taking life for granted? Living a soul-filled life? Our courage to examine this week or certain months provides the telltale signs. Are we dismissing, ignoring, or procreating the intentional desires and our irrefutable and positive outcomes?

~~Our' world is teeming with the decoys or obvious temptations. Veer off course. Wander down a one-way street. Be a clone. Hang tight with a clique, just like the notorious adolescent years. It is a historic avenue when we rise above and abandon our tiresome or monotonous footprints. The "now" is a real time and place to abandon those monotonous footprints in our "new normal" history and antiquity.

~~Presentness and a perceptiveness are awesome virtues for any change in our lifespan promenade. These attributes replace our mesa-mesa roadways, the offbeat routes, and those one-way streets. Living in the "now" becomes a fortuitous moment for our preference of a brand-new avenue or an intriguing route.

~~Swerve out the way in the nick of time. Avoid gridlock. Make a couple of pit stops. Feel the difference of energy and our get-up-and-go initiative? In our "new normal" world—Are we triggering the baby steps or making a decision to launch the quantum leaps with our initiatives?

~~Mind, body, and spirit cannot be separated. Ah, makes common sense. Then roll out the famous red carpet—for a grand debut and the induction of this holistic spirit. Our forever-guardians like the synergy of this aura and a prosperous karma. Put out that good karma and the "positive vibrations" for an unsettled world.

~~Transparency is just that—not less, not more. Let yourself know yourself. Like other committed mortals, the soul-filled journey takes off from our launch pad. What an inauguration!

~~Shun our fears and those stinging or nagging doubts. Rid our ego of the incessant mind-chatter. Experience the truths that turn up and drop anchor. Embrace and tap into a fearless attitude and stunning altitude. Humanitarian precedents and lessons abound every day—our tapping into the gutsy, heroic endeavors and the valiant altitudes.

~~Slow down. Let this repetition become sublime, smashingly good for our soul. Slow down again. Let this healing-ritual emerge, a real freedom from any of our self-sabotage and our imposing judgements. Manifest this healing-ritual and this evolution for our global world.

~~I choose never to forget… Walk barefoot in a forest emitting the fragrances from the lofty pines, the aromatic cedars, and the quaking aspens. Allow plentiful layers of relaxation and the restoration seep into the meridian flows of our body. Unite with Mother Earth in this forest of a natural aromatherapy. Entrust our bare feet to unearth a pristine beauty, the vibrations, and the synchrony of a soul-filled spirit. I am soul-filled, as I still walk "close to home" and into those resplendent "vibrations" of Mother Earth Gaia.

~~Abundance comes to fruition with a daily commitment to discovery learning. Nurturing that momentum begets a positive mindset, if and when we allow the symbolic fruits to ripen. We human beings exude a continual mindfulness each and every day of our pandemic. We do not reject or banish the glimmers of hope and the ultimate optimism for our future.

~~Credible professionals talk and write about the "free spirit" individuals. They go with the flow and own that choice. Decisions include a risk-taking, regardless of any notorious pit in the stomach. Their faith and the trust? Their mindset and their intuition? Living with any imminent regrets is a worse prospect, gamble, or another pitfall. During our worldly upheavals and transitions, the personal "lifetime lessons" still reappear with the clear intentions and a courageous pursuit of our unique pathways.

~~Watch an exceptional television program or a compelling movie. Does immediate immersion and forgetting the time of day occur? Praise and honor these unanticipated delights and all-consuming, gripping appeals. Repeating this daily or weekly option—sooner than later—is the happy chance, a blessing, and the "serendipity" at the best-ever altitude.

~~No arbitrary or haphazard reasons. No flukes. No gimmicks. No Cinderella or Prince Charming wishes to come hither. Rightful planning, a solid predisposition, and a positive catalyst to live a soul-filled life takes our potpourri of gutsy actions. This medley includes any dark abyss that flies in the face of one's capacity and a genuine power to latch onto our forthcoming and triumphant glories.

~~Radiate a loving-kindness. Let that sentiment of good will and propensity ooze from every pore. Watch the quality difference that arises in someone's life—the stranger, an acquaintance, your best friend, or a beloved partner.

~~A longtime friend listened to my health story with the facial expressions of an authentic love. The expressions became a mirror image that boosted that day and our soul-filled hearts. Each of us accepts again and again—to procreate our legacy of an endearing friendship or an unmistakable love.

~~Let the music play. Tunes are therapeutic to our souls. I was comfy, a Zen-like figurine on my couch, enjoying the writing and my tunes. Near the CD player were loving-memory cards with Robert Frost's prose. "Two roads diverged in a wood, and I—I took the one less travelled by. And that has made all the difference." Composing on my lap top, I paused for a break, when I heard a rendition by Michael Buble' of a song entitled, "All of Me." Deciding to stand in front of my parental pictures and the loving memory cards, I felt a solace. "All of Me" was my parents' favorite song, always a sing-a-long and their time for a dance. As children and even as adults, we joined in the dance spirit. No coincidence. My parents, an inner solace, and my inspired writing—all of this gifting, while I was "staying at home."

Seeking imprints of the transformations in our wanton times...
Honoring a dignity of personal commitments to our daily connections...
Believing in the radiant light, forthcoming with our abundance...

Epilogue

My first writings for *Epiphanies* and recent additions to each chapter are complete in the "now" that any of us embrace in early June, 2020. Our world pandemic, the rising or flat-lined indicators, the respected front-liners, and our future are in the "stay tuned" phases. My book is headed forward with its publication in the early summer. There were unique moments to honor in the "now." I persevered, remaining hopeful throughout my journey. Gratitude still resonates.

This evening and our tomorrows? Hope floats with me—in this "now" and whatever lies ahead for our future. So this epilogue still resonates my continuum of hope and the optimism.

There is a season—for all things—beautiful and transcendental. There is a tempo, triggering the moments of synchrony. Perfect? Well, a likelihood of the unforeseeable and idyllic timing for healing is as close as possible to those "perfect imperfections" and a completeness.

Our high-tone genetics, taking wellness to another level, our humanitarian efforts, and lessening the daily stressors are our endowments or blessings. There is our mindset of the positive beliefs and an optimism. There is ambitious research on the cusp of anticipated and the contemporary, scientific discoveries. Each of these considerations opens a gateway or the portals to our societal anticipation and a melange of personal hopes.

Our attitude of gratitude and honor is unconcealed. None of us is capable of seeing the supreme handwriting on the wall. None of us secures the absolute truths. We cannot prophesy or fathom—our exact lifeline to Mother Earth Gaia.

All of these realisms create the down-to-earth realms for our forthcoming contemplations. The bottom line of "not knowing" an absolute time clock on Mother Earth begins to actualize in our core being. The societal cliche—it is what it is—starts a unique momentum for our global efforts.

Our mind, body, and spirit give birth to processing this "real or surreal world" and "how things are." We mediate, gather, and take a stand. When we decide upon an acceptance, it is evidenced by our substantial and intrinsic actions.

Chip away, knock oneself out, or go all out. Many kindred spirits favor the choice to expend an influential energy and the earnest efforts. Our mass media and technology keep us abreast. Ultimately, there is a daily consciousness to strive and do our best. "Our best" keeps coming forth.

We "zero in" with a credible process called the "assimilation and accommodation" of our world. The novel passages, any shortcuts, and the directions that appear on our horizon are meant to be. Destiny, good karma, and a quintessential providence begin to meld into our daily living.

Our adaptations are realized and buttoned up. Done deal? We still strive for more answers. Something else happens. Another contemporary cliche'—being comfortable in one's own skin—makes its unforgettable debut. We covet this new consciousness, especially as our "emotional intelligence" and practice heightens and evolves with our native intelligence.

Ownership becomes a series of noteworthy actions, not just today's popular jargon. A sense of humor—the lighthearted facets of our persona—are equally important allies during our global pandemic. We value our virtual tours and our connections with the comedians at home, virtual musical events with regional, national, and international celebrities, and other esteemed individuals who provide the hopeful renewals and the enlightening messages.

Whatever earthly time that any human being is granted, there is one affirmation that endures, perching and inhabiting our being. The "now" is what each one of us "knows" for sure.

Yesterday or tomorrow? Nanoseconds or hours? Weeks, different months, or the next one or two years? Our reception and acceptance of the "unknown or absolute timing" on Mother Earth transposes into a colorful, an unequalled, and our intangible wealth.

We dignify and honor the abundance with our re-awakenings and a heartfelt unity. We enjoy a pure essence of that intangible wealth and today's moments…

Day-by-Day Journaling

How I am mindful of my daily connections, remotely or in-person,
with the "social distancing" and the "staying at home"…

Day-by-Day Journaling

How I am mindful of my personal epiphanies and my re-awakenings…

Day-by-Day Journaling

How I am mindful of my envisioning a harmony and the unity for our global world…

Printed in the United States
By Bookmasters